Windows to World's Religions

Windows to World's Religions

Selected Proceedings of
The Global Congress on the World's Religions
After September 11

Edited by
Arvind Sharma

D.K. Printworld (P) Ltd.
New Delhi

Cataloging in Publication Data — DK

[Courtesy: D.K. Agencies (P) Ltd. <docinfo@dkagencies.com>]

Global Congress on World's Religions After September 11 (2006 : Montreal, Canada)

Windows to world's religions : selected proceedings of the Global Congress on the World's Religions After September 11 / edited by Arvind Sharma.

p. cm.

Includes bibliographical references.

Includes index.

ISBN 13: 9788124604755

ISBN 10: 8124604754

1. Religions – History – 21st century – Congresses. 2. Religions – Relations – Congresses. 3. September 11 Terrorist Attacks, 2001 – Religious aspects – Congresses. 4. Human rights – Religious aspects – Congresses. I. Sharma, Arvind, 1940- II. Title.

DDC 200.905 22

ISBN13: 978-81-246-0475-5

ISBN10: 81-246-0475-4

First published in India in 2009

Published and printed by:

D.K. Printworld (P) Ltd.

Regd. office : *"Sri Kunj'*, F-52, Bali Nagar

Ramesh Nagar Metro Station

New Delhi - 110 015

Phones : (011) 2545 3975; 2546 6019; *Fax* : (011) 2546 5926

E-mail: dkprintworld@vsnl.net

Web: www.dkprintword.com

Contents

PANELS
No. 1: Journey into Openness

No. 2: Responsibility Beyond Borders

Introduction

Arvind Sharma

THE events of September 11, 2001 are etched in the collective consciousness of our generation and ineffaceable from modern memory. They also brought to the fore the issue of the role of religion in the present-day world. A global congress on World's Religions After September 11 was held in Montreal from 11-15 September 2006 to explore this issue further and to examine whether religion could *also* be a force for good, notwithstanding the current opprobrium which attaches to it. A total of 225 speakers participated in over 8 workshops, 18 plenary sessions, 47 panels and 236 individual presentations over the five days of this congress, which attracted 2025 participants from 84 countries.

I hope the readers will welcome the sampling of the material presented at this congress, now offered through the medium of this volume. It also includes the text of the Universal Declaration of Human Rights, which was released at this congress for discussion in the academic and faith communities.

1

Polyphony and the Aesthetics of Interreligious Dialogue

John N. Sheveland

CHRISTIAN encounters with other religious traditions are often plagued by one especially regrettable feature. The theology of religions school has provided Christians the opportunity to speculate on the salvific relevance of other religious traditions and, in many instances, to be wonderfully and appropriately inclusive of religious others. While such speculation certainly has its place within the theological guild, a caution is in order. The theology of religions school risks training us to consider religions reductively in terms of their alleged truthfulness or non-truthfulness with respect to revelation and soteriology. In other words, we have been trained implicitly to reduce religions to our judgements concerning their truth claims, so that our interlocutors and their beliefs exist for us within pre-determined rubrics we choose to recognize as familiar, or worse, within the confines of our a priori judgement on their truth claims. This procedure both reifies and narrows our grasp of other religious paths and obfuscates relationships with religious neighbours.[1]

1. For criticisms of theologies of religions for the alleged domestication of other religions, particularly of the models Paul Knitter has labelled the "fulfilment model" of inclusivism and →

Because of such inhibition of true dialogue, comparative theologians like Francis X. Clooney and James Fredericks have called for a moratorium on theologies of religions.[2]

This essay adopts and builds on the thesis of Clooney, Fredericks, and other comparative theologians who desire to learn from our religious neighbours by postponing—if not jettisoning—judgements about our neighbours' truth claims as a preliminary and necessary step towards engaging neighbours in their irreducible particularity. To this end I suggest the musical aural image of "polyphony" as one possible model by which to envision the complex work of Christian comparative theology. A theological appropriation of musical polyphony bears fruit by reorienting the theological task as conceived in the theologian's imagination. The reorientation consists in a call away from judgement of others to the appreciation of them, from comparison predicated on competition to comparison predicated on aesthetic appreciation. In short, polyphony prizes theological aesthetics

---

→ the "mutuality model" of pluralism, and for their alleged inhibition of genuine dialogue, see: S. Mark Heim, *Salvations: Truth and Difference in Religions* (Maryknoll: Orbis, 1995), pp. 13-43, 211-30; and Michael L. Barnes, S.J., *Theology and the Dialogue of Religions* (Cambridge: Cambridge University, 2002), pp. 3-28. For the response of a leading advocate of the mutuality model of pluralism which attempts to redress these criticisms, see Paul F. Knitter, "Catholics and Other Religions: Bridging the Gap Between Dialogue and Theology," *Louvain Studies* 24 (1999), pp. 319-54.

2. See Francis X. Clooney, *Theology After Vedanta* (Albany: SUNY, 1993); James Fredericks, *Faith Among Faiths* (Mahwah: Paulist, 1999); and *Buddhists and Christians: Through Comparative Theology to Solidarity* (Maryknoll: Orbis, 2004), p. 99. I recommend an ordering principle whereby the performance of comparative theological inquiry creates the conditions for the possibility of a theology of religions, however conceived, rather than eliminating the school and the questions it seeks to address.

over antagonism.[3]

In what follows I elaborate three broad proposals concerning a theological appropriation of musical polyphony:

1. Polyphony preserves a distinction-in-unity among the theological voices being compared.
2. Polyphony contributes an aesthetic image and vocabulary to assist the comparativist's construal of theological subject matter, thus training our theological "ear" to appreciate and be edified by our religious neighbours.
3. Polyphony contributes a new metaphor by which to imagine the corporate membership and solidarity of religious speakers within this religiously diverse global community.

Polyphony Allows for Distinction-in-unity

The musical genre of polyphony — also called counterpoint — flourished in the Renaissance and Baroque periods in the Latin West. Quite appropriately, it evolved from the medieval style of harmonized chant called *Organum*, the sung prayer of Christian monks. Polyphony literally means "many voices," and a composer in this genre would deliberately bring together multiple voices singing their own individual melody lines.[4] It is important to note that each voice, rather than being a mere

---

3. In addition to my own dissertation, *Creatures in Correspondence: The Unity of Piety and Responsibility in Karl Rahner, Karl Barth, and Vedanta Desika* (2006) UMI Number: 3209830, the only experiment with polyphony in the fields of theology and religious studies of which I am aware is: Mark E. Biddle, *Polyphony and Symphony in Prophetic Literature: Rereading Jeremiah 7-20*, Studies in Old Testament Interpretation 2 (Macon, GA: Mercer University, 1996).

4. Leading composers included Jacob Obrecht (d.1505), Josquin de Prez (d. 1521), Giovanni Pierluigi da Palestrina (d. 1594), and William Byrd (d. 1623).

harmonic part in relationship to a dominant melody, represents a distinct melody with its own integrity and musical logic. The melody could remain independent. But in this genre, melody lines are combined deliberately to produce an emergent structure of greater depth than any single melody line could produce on its own. John Rain remarks that:

> It is hard to write a beautiful song. It is even harder to write several individually beautiful songs that, when sung simultaneously, sound as a more beautiful polyphonic whole.[5]

Here, Rain suggests that the combination of multiple melodies, beautiful individually in their own right, can give rise to more beauty which one could not have perceived in temporally isolated soundings of the melodies. Multiple melody lines superimposed on each other collaborate to create a polyphonic whole more beautiful than the sum of its parts. Rain continues with a remark comparative theologians would be eager to hear:

> The internal structures that create each of the voices, separately must contribute to the emergent structure of the polyphony, which in turn must reinforce and comment on the structures of the individual voices. The way that is accomplished in detail is . . . "counterpoint."[6]

Not only do individual voices when combined give rise to a more beautiful emergent structure. That emergent structure also bends back, reflexively, as a whole that now sheds further light on the individual voices comprising it. The emergent structure, or polyphonic chord, offers the hearer a new vantage point, a new aural context or set of resources with which to

---

5. John Rain, *Music Inside and Out: Going too Far in Musical Essays* (Singapore: G+B Arts International, 2001), p. 177.

6. Ibid.

appreciate the individual voices. That new vantage point affords unexpected insight into the previously isolated voices. Rather than assaulting the ear with a kind of cacophony or discord, polyphony instead reveals the character and depth of individual voices in a way only it can. Parallel motifs, tensions, and disagreements are sharpened. A previously unobserved quality in a given melody line now shines more clearly on account of a separate melody line creating counterpoint, drawing out its quality by way of contrasting with it. The contrast or tension among the voices serves as a pedagogical tool training the ear to appreciate both the emergent structure and the irreducible particularity of the voices constituting that structure. To articulate the point in negative terms, one hears a comparatively impoverished version of a given melody line when that melody remains isolated within its own logic.

Transposing all of this to a comparative theological discussion involves recognizing that an audience understands an individual religious speaker better when her speech is heard collectively in a shared context with other speeches. Polyphony resists the temptation to caricature other voices or pass over their real differences. Those engaged in comparative theology or interreligious dialogues know that the acknowledgement of difference is a *sine qua non* for engaging the other with hospitality.[7] Polyphony thus assists us with the moral imperative of taking our interlocutors seriously precisely in their differences from us.

These two features of polyphony — recognition of differences and attention to an emergent structure of intelligibility — are the same features prized by comparative

---

7. For more on the application of hospitality to the encounter with religious "strangers," see: Martin Marty, *When Faiths Collide* (Oxford: Blackwell, 2004), pp. 124-48.

theologians. On the one hand, comparative theologians wish to underscore the real differences, contrasts, and tensions between voices in order to resist domestication and caricature. On the other hand, they are keenly interested in the possible emergence of a broad, unitive framework of intelligibility making comparison both possible and desirable. Polyphony encourages the comparativist to pursue both tasks.

Polyphony Amplifies the Aesthetic Dimension of Theological Comparison

If polyphony can be imported into comparative theological method, it would offer a completely new style of theological dialogue and discourse. That new tone, I suggest, will give rise to a renewed appreciation of the aesthetic or affective qualities of our texts and traditions. The overworked speculations concerning the status of another religion's truth claims *vis-à-vis* those of one's own would be less urgent and replaced by a readiness to be edified by the dialogue and the learning it produces.

Musical polyphony involves multiple melody lines combined in a non-competitive fashion. No one voice occupies the melody line to the exclusion of other voices. Rather, each voice counts as a melody, none of which should overpower the others. Precedence and subsequence are replaced by musical dynamics such as augmentation and diminution, which focus the audience on contextual dynamics. The analogy with comparative theology is clear. Transportation of this motif to comparative theology suggests that no one speaker should be self-preoccupied in ways that exclude other voices or which precondition the dialogue. Rival truth claims may be of interest in the distant future, but only after the laborious work of comparison takes place. While the theologian is making comparisons and learning from her colleagues in other traditions, she does well to consider the affective or aesthetic component of comparison; she does well to let herself be schooled by the dialogue of which she is a part. It is not a dialogue over which she exercises control. It is instead a dialogue of unpredictable development and perhaps surprising edification. She is at the disposal of the dialogue; the dialogue is not at her disposal. And this dialogue can, just like polyphony, be marked by a great complexity of voices educating the careful listener, and it can also be marked by great tension begging for resolution. She will perceive this tension and recognize its place in the theological community as voices contributing to a complex score of music.

Her task, moreover, difficult and painstaking though it may be, will be to compose or intellectually organize polyphony from the voices present. She, as a composer-theologian, will be responsible for deducing moments of harmony as well as discord, in each case explaining how this is so and what the relationships between voices reveal about those same voices.

Polyphony Contributes a New Metaphor by which to Imagine the Corporate Membership of all (Individual Melodies) within a Global Community (a Polyphonic Score of Music) of Religious Reflection

This third thesis suggests that theological speakers are bound together in a common enterprise or symphony *because of* their diversity, which has now become not a problem to be solved or overcome but a richness to be explored. Theological speculation can be seen now as the aesthetic and possibly edifying endeavour it is, as an endeavour in which all participate and contribute to the beauty of the whole. My neighbour contributes to my own self-understanding and helps me to locate myself in solidarity with the global community of theological reflection. Our differences and distinctions no longer relegate us to a competitive zero-sum game but rather are housed together under a larger rubric of unity, though not identification.

This change in the perception of religious difference is immense. If this sort of corporate endeavour seizes the theological imagination, the prospects for interreligious learning and conflict resolution are encouraging. The change in perception would spell humility in the best sense of the word: an awareness of our individual limits and gifts coupled with a willingness to learn from others who have now become resources ignored at our own peril.

A virtue or duty from Catholic Social Teaching which may help to describe this symphony of interdependence is solidarity. In the framework of Catholic Social Teaching, solidarity points to a thick species of empathy or an attitude of togetherness with the other predicated precisely on the experience of interdependence that characterizes modern persons in the world today. While solidarity is a virtue which all persons can understand and enact, the depth of its meaning is to be found in qualities of Christian faith and life which regard one's neighbour "as the living image of God the Father, redeemed by Jesus Christ, and placed under the action of the Holy Spirit."[8] To date, the elaboration of solidarity in Catholic Social Teaching, especially by John Paul II, has privileged the political and economic interdependence of human persons and societies, linking it tightly with social, economic, and political justice. Yet the virtue of solidarity can also obtain meaningfully in the arena of interreligious dialogue, which also observes the interdependence of persons and recommends a disposition or spirituality by which they should view and receive "others." Such solidarity, with its conception of individual persons as responsible relationships between self, neighbours, remote neighbours, and even nature itself, is no doubt urgently

---

8. Charles E. Curran, Kenneth R. Himes, and Thomas A. Shannon, "Sollicitudo rei socialis (On Social Concern)," in Kenneth R. Himes, ed., *Modern Catholic Social Teaching* (Washington, D.C.: Georgetown University Press, 2005), p. 429.

needed in today's troubled religious climate.[9] Polyphony thus offers an interdisciplinary metaphor by which to imagine the application of solidarity to interreligious dialogue, illuminating perhaps another dimension to the meaning of social justice.

Conclusion by Way of Caution

In one sense, an interdisciplinary offering of this sort greatly complicates matters and places demands on those who would apply it to theological reflection. While this example of polyphony functions to reinvest comparative theological discourse with aesthetics, effect, edification, and solidarity, it also brings with it some potential stumbling blocks. I list three of these now as a caution to myself and others and as an initial indicator of nuance yet to be teased out if the metaphor is to achieve the full relevance proposed above.

Superficiality. It will not do to enlist an interdisciplinary model superficially and without adequate compliance to the demands of music as an independent field of original application. The theologian-composer will need to acquire a working knowledge of polyphony, including its historical antecedents and ecclesial context, which musicologists could both recognize and endorse.

Incommensurability. Neither in music nor in comparative theology is polyphony designed to tolerate an unlimited degree of difference. Where difference can be organized and understood as polyphony, we need theologian-composers adept at deducing harmonic depth in the voices being compared. But where it cannot, we need theologian-composers who skillfully apply theological norms to determine the line of demarcation between, on the one hand, differences that together create polyphonic harmony and, on the other, differences which together lack resolution and are discordant.

9. Ibid., p. 427.

Not all tension can or should find resolution. How does comparative theology navigate the important demands of theological norms while nonetheless dialoguing with our neighbours in hospitality and solidarity? Here and elsewhere a theology of religions is appropriate if Christian comparative theology is to maintain the normative quality implied in its first adjective.

Reception. How will my religious neighbours and all people of goodwill receive my construal of their voices according to this metaphor? Is this interdisciplinary musing, like so much theology to date, plagued by a Western cultural imperialism, however aesthetic? Theologian-composers will need to tend to the concerns that this method prioritises a norm alien to the traditions to which it is being applied and that it is just one more cloaked version of a Western or Christian imperialism indifferent to the perception of those to whom the metaphor is meant peaceably to apply. Otherwise, a metaphor proposed for its irenic qualities may ironically give rise to the antagonism it seeks to avoid.

Verification and Multiple Attestation. The merit of polyphony as a comparative methodology will stand or fall on the basis of its capacity to organize and characterize the dynamics of comparative theological experiments in ways illuminating and meaningful. Comparative theologians will need to apply this interdisciplinary metaphor to actual comparisons and test its fitness and capacity to organize independent voices in dialogue with each other. Such experiments may deal in highly specific subject matter, in which case the metaphor will prove useful if shown to pass the test of multiple attestation, that is, if it can be shown to organize and characterize multiple sets of discrete comparisons sharing minimal overlap in subject matter. Such potential for multiple attestation will speak to the fitness of this interdisciplinary metaphor as a template on which comparative theological inquiry can rest. It will also recommend polyphony to other theologians intent on entering into dialogue with a conciliatory bias which nonetheless attends to the irreducible particularity of theological voices and construes that same particularity as a resource for the interlocutor's own self-understanding. The method of polyphony will thus contribute an interdisciplinary metaphor by which theologians can perceive theological differences in terms of aesthetics rather than antagonism.[10]

---

10. The author thanks Roger D. Haight, S.J. and Roger O. Doyle, D.M.A. for their comments.

2

Spirituality as the Root of Tolerance: Religion Practised at the Retreat Centre

Paul Schwartzentruber

When the gods have fled the temple, they never return.

— *Carl Jung*

A quest, I think, is essentially open-ended. It is very different from a confirmation of a given faith as well as from the gratification of one's spiritual needs. A quest is not like a search, say, for one's misplaced keys, where what is to be found is known in advance and merely not at hand; it is not merely a process of personally actualizing for oneself generally or collectively known answers. The outcome of a quest, if it is a real one, is not known ahead of time.

— *Wolfgang Giegerich*[1]

I WANT to reflect on one of the major trajectories of contemporary religious experience in North America, namely, what is commonly (and journalistically) referred to as "spirituality." In doing so, I want to try to add some (much-needed) precision to our understanding of the phenomenon as a category of religious self-understanding. A major point of reference for this reflection will be the equally vibrant phenomenon of fundamentalism. Spirituality and fundamentalism are not only obvious points of contrast, however, they are also natural twins, born into the (historical-sociological) family of

1. http://www.guildofpastoralpsychology.org.uk/page9.html

modernity, secularization and the post-modern social order characterized by "connectivity" rather than commitment, a "liquidity of life politics" and "communities of occasion" (rather than of sameness).[2] This common ancestry and growth together in the post-modern context asks for a more nuanced and experiential analysis of both phenomena, it seems to me. Moreover, this analysis must highlight the very ancient religious problem of identity and the tolerance for difference, which has become violently urgent again in the post-modern context.

This last claim draws its impetus from experience in the new religious "marketplace" that is the North American retreat centre.[3] The retreat centre becomes a valuable, new locus of reflection on both spirituality and fundamentalism because their encounter there has become "public," Inter-religious and dialogic in nature. In each sense, the retreat centre has drawn the religious experience (whether spirituality or fundamentalism) out of the isolated context of a religious tradition/community defined by physical or ideological boundaries and out of more or less privatized spheres of self-definition, into a space where a tolerance of difference and the traditional features of identity are constantly "reformed and reforming." All of this makes it a place of creative encounter between religious traditions and their "orphaned" spiritualities and fundamentalisms. Having said this much, it should also be clear that the retreat centre becomes a peculiar

---

2. Zygmunt Bauman, *Liquid Love*, p. 35: "The "communities of sameness", pre-determined but waiting to be revealed and filled with substance, are giving way to "communities of occasion", expected to self-compose around events, idols, panics or fashions: most diverse as focal points, yet sharing the trait of short, and shortening, life expectation."

3. Since 1997, I have been the Director of Marguerite Centre, a Roman Catholic Retreat Centre in Pembroke, Ont., Canada. I will say more on this context below.

place of refuge for adherents of both kinds precisely in that time after "the gods have fled the temple." The nature of this time and the reasons for the peculiar "refuge" merit some reflection at the outset.

Spirituality and Fundamentalism as Orphans of Religion

One meaning of Jung's very pregnant epithet is that all religious traditions have experienced a fundamental "demystifying" of the temple/sacred space of the natural world during the passage into the modern world.[4] The metaphor of the "gods leaving the temple," however, corresponds to that deeper experience of modern consciousness which "imagines losing its gods, whereas in reality we have been removed from the place where we can experience them."[5] This exile of modern consciousness from sacred space and from an "original innocence" of religious experience is surely the most clear feature and burden of all of contemporary religious self-understanding.[6] Yet it is crucial to be clear that what has been lost through this exile is not religious experience or practice (which continue to thrive

4. W. Giegerich "Rupture, Or: Psychology and Religion," in W. Giegerich, *The Neurosis of Psychology: Primary Papers towards a Critical Psychology*, (New Orleans: Spring Journal Books, 2005), pp. 226-27: "The natural world as a whole no longer is the sphere in which we (logically and psychologically) dwell and which surrounds us fundamentally. . . . There has been a fundamental change. The "same' sun that man saw 3000 years ago is no longer the same. We can no longer *legitimately* speak of a sunrise, as in mythic times, let alone *see* the God or Goddess in it".
5. Giegerich, "Rupture," p. 226.
6. Cf., P. Ricoeur, *The Symbolism of Evil*, (Boston: Beacon, 1960), p. 351: "I believe that being can still speak to me — no longer, of course, under the precritical form of immediate belief, but as the second immediacy aimed at by hermeneutics. . . . This second naivete. . . ."

everywhere) but religion as a "level of consciousness," religion as the psychic embodiment of a meaningful answer to the question of the world.[7] Thus "desacralization" or secularization not only means that the modern human being can no longer experience "the cosmos as a whole [as] . . . an organism [which is] *real, living, and sacred* . . .", but also and primarily that "the world to which religions were answers has, as it were, moved out from under them," and become an artefact, an abandoned temple.[8]

It is in this sense that both spirituality and fundamentalism can and should be considered post-modern orphans of their various religious traditions, that is, forms of religious practice and experience in exile from the sacred space of the temple and therefore from a direct and logical religious connection/relation to the "world."[9] This means, on the one hand, that spirituality and fundamentalism are, obviously, essentially "public" phenomena in the post-modern world (i.e. in exile

---

7. Giegerich, "Rupture," p. 228 "I do not think that religions (as personal faith, as literal practices) are threatened today; on the contrary, they enjoy increasing popularity. What is threatened, however, is that logical status or level of consciousness of which religion is the embodiment. . . . Now a changed world, one that exists on the post-natural subatomic level, represents a totally new "question"."
8. Mircea Eliade, *The Sacred and the Profane: The Nature of Religion* (New York: Harcourt Brace , Jovanovich, 1959), p. 117; Giegerich, 227: "We are now confronted with a logically entirely new world, to which religion no longer corresponds."
9. On Fundamentalism cf., Wikipedia, "Fundamentalism": "Fundamentalism is therefore a movement through which the adherents attempt to rescue religious identity from absorption into modern, Western culture, where this absorption appears to the enclave to have made irreversible progress in the wider religious community, necessitating the assertion of a separate identity based upon the fundamental or founding principles of the religion."

from any particular sacred place): they both reside "outside" the traditional boundaries of the religious community (and religion *per se*) in an essential way.[10] On the other hand, it also means that, as such, they are also very much disconnected from the levels of consciousness (scientific, economic, political) that interpret "reality/meaning" on the "post-natural, subatomic level." At best, they have come to expression in marginal communities of "cognitive dissonance," who lay claim — against the grain of science, politics, and economics — to the still-unexplained human need (for salvation) or some ever-greater realm of mystery.[11] So both spirituality and fundamentalism are — in an entirely novel sense — "in and yet not-of" the post-modern world. From this uneasy relation to it, they find a natural if peculiar refuge in the retreat centre.

The Retreat Centre

I want to say something next about the nature of the retreat centre and this by way of a brief history.

A Google search will turn up several sites listing what are approximately 1500 retreat centres in Canada and the US. Approximately half of these are Christian (Buddhist is the next largest group) and three-fourths of those, Roman Catholic.[12] That is natural, if one recognizes the long-standing historical connection with communities of religious men and

---

10. This is obvious enough for spirituality — perhaps less so for fundamentalism, until one recognizes how readily, for example, the Pentecostal (fundamentalist) makes common cause with the Roman Catholic (fundamentalist) and that, both in the political and theological realm. I will develop this claim further below.
11. Richard Antoun, *Understanding Fundamentalism: Christian, Islamic, and Jewish Movements* (Walnut Creek, CA: AltaMira Press, 2001), describes fundamentalism as "a cognitive and affective orientation to the modern world" (p. 153)
12. See http://www.retreatsintl.org/list.htm for the list of most of these.

women whose large buildings and age-old traditions of hospitality really gave birth to the notion of the retreat centre in the first place. These retreat centres really came to rise and flourish in the late 1960s and 1970s as a result of the reforms of the Second Vatican Council. These were conceived largely as places for "renewal," that is, for passing on to a hitherto often passive laity, the message and meaning of its liturgical and theological reforms according to a new and engaged model of adult education. This model established itself as a kind of hallmark and touchstone — attracting to the retreat centre other movements with similar aims: the 12-step traditions of Alcoholics Anonymous, various movements committed to social justice and political education, and a variety of "encounter groups" intended to develop interpersonal skills in a religious or humanistic context (Cursillo, Marriage Encounter, etc.). Finally, to this dynamic model of adult education, the religious communities themselves contributed two further, crucial streams: (1) out of communities of religious sisters primarily came a focus on women's self-discovery which drew on radically new Inter-religious, psychological and mythical resources (from the Enneagram to Jungian analysis to Celtic Spirituality) and (2) from the same communities came a newly reconceived practice of spiritual direction which drew largely on the Jesuit traditions of Ignatian spirituality.

The retreat centres that housed these eclectic practices and interests quickly found themselves faced with questions of tolerance and of religious identity. These questions were made the more urgent by the rise of "new age" spiritualism in the 1970s, as well as by the flourishing of various Sufi, Hindu and Buddhist spiritual practices in North American culture during the same period. In what would become a very significant development, retreat centres addressed these questions primarily, not by drawing on their traditional sources of religious identity (e.g. which at that time were themselves being hotly debated within Roman Catholicism), but rather by pointing outward to a common ground emerging in part around the new model of adult education and moral development represented by the work of Piaget and Kohlberg.[13] This was a practical rather than a theoretical decision: by practising hospitality to an increasingly diverse array of spiritual practices, retreat centres turned toward — indeed, in many cases, gave shape to — a spirituality of personal growth and transformation that had already moved beyond many of the traditional boundaries of religious identity.

In these historical terms, it is possible to argue that Roman Catholic retreat centres made a most significant contribution to the development of the phenomenon of "spirituality" as we have come to know it. As centres of experiential, adult learning, they drew together practices from many traditional religious sources and drew as well on emerging psychological and sociological insights and techniques. One thinks, for example, of the widespread popularity of personality models such as Myers-Briggs (with its Jungian framework) and the Enneagram (with its Sufi roots) — in addition to the model of 12-step practices mentioned above. Retreat centres gave place for that kind of programming and in doing so brought it into a vibrant dialogue with the Catholic and Celtic practices of "spiritual direction." At the same time, figures like the Benedictine John Main, the Jesuit Fr. Anthony de Mello as well as the Cistercian Thomas Keating were building bridges between Buddhist and Hindu practices of meditation and the ancient Christian tradition of hesychastic prayer.[14] This work

13. Cf. for a sense of the spectrum of that debate see the work of Hans Küng, Leonardo Boff and David Tracy.

14. Wikipedia, "Christian Meditation," Dom John Main (1926-82) learned *mantra* meditation from Swāmi Satyānanda in Malaya. Swāmi Satyānanda told him he must do "Christian meditation" →

happened in and because of the open — exploratory — space of the retreat centre and it led to ongoing groups that continue in North American retreat centres until the present. Finally, as the sponsoring religious communities became more focused on a social justice agenda (through influence of liberation theology, Catholic social teaching and most recently eco-theology), retreat centres have become increasingly creative and innovative in the development of the social, political and ecological dimensions of spirituality (via the work of Matthew Fox, Thomas Berry et al.). This too brought a significant broadening of spiritual practice and set it in frameworks far broader than those provided by traditional theology (e.g. the new cosmos story).

It is important to note that all of this Inter-religious weaving was happening on the level of practice and as a kind of experiential dialogue — in that sense, it obviated both traditional dogmatic definitions of identity and also the slow-working processes of ecumenical and interreligious dialogue. By the same token, it raised the question of how this emerging and eclectic set of spiritual practices happening within and

→ and so John Main used the *mantra* Maranatha, which is Aramaic for "Come, Lord", as in I Corinthians 16:22 and Revelation 22:20. Dom John Main later found parallels with John Cassian's (fourth century) mention of the repetition of a short verse as a focus for prayer. Fr Laurence Freeman continues Dom John Main's work. Wikipedia, "Anthony de Mello". Until his sudden death on 2 June 1987, Fr. Tony de Mello was the director of the Sadhana Institute of Pastoral Counselling near Poona, India. Author of five best selling books, renowned worldwide for his workshops, retreats, and prayer courses, he aimed simply to teach people HOW TO PRAY, how to WAKE UP AND LIVE. Cf., T.K. Thomas, *The Prayer of the Frog Called into Question,* for a good summary of de Mello's work and his search for a "radically ecumenical spirituality". Wikipedia, "Thomas Keating" (b. 1923) is a Cistercian monk, priest, and abbot. He was born in New York City, and attended Deerfield Academy, Yale University, and Fordham University, graduating in December 1943. He is a founder of the Centering Prayer movement and of Contemplative Outreach, Ltd.

from the Catholic tradition would define itself in relation to traditional, ecclesial Catholicism. Doctrinal condemnations of Matthew Fox and Tony DeMello (as well as the Vatican's Instruction on New Age Spirituality) only heightened this problem of self-definition.

All of this is to say that the retreat centre is a clearly post-modern, religious phenomenon or locale — certainly not a "temple" with its emphasis on orthodoxy or orthopraxy — but experiential in nature and — precisely because of its commitment to the open-ended and self-directed process of adult (self-) education — also by nature essentially creative and experimental. What happens there is more clearly what Giegerich calls a spiritual "quest." I want to hasten to add that this does not mean that the retreat centre is without a religious commitment or focus or a faithful rootedness in a religious tradition (Though from some fundamentalist positions which equate education with evangelism, that is exactly what it seems). To explain this, however, we must return to the notions of spirituality and fundamentalism as post-modern orphans of "the abandoned temple" of religion.

The Spectrum of Spirituality and Fundamentalism

Neither spirituality nor fundamentalism can stand in the place of classical, pre-modern religious belief and practice. Indeed, despite various claims to the contrary, that position is simply no longer available to us, to any of us. "When the gods have fled the temple, *they never return*."

What is available is a spectrum of religious experience and self-understanding that can be traced between two basic and creative possibilities: spirituality and fundamentalism.[15] Let me start with the latter to explain what I mean.

---

15. I offer this analysis in the spirit of the late Cardinal Bernadin who sought to find the "common ground" underlying religious polarity.

Fundamentalism builds its identity around the claim to constitute a kind of renewed and distinct "religious enclave" faithful to (so-called) "fundamental beliefs and practices that have been abandoned by the larger religious group" from which it comes.[16] Since that abandonment of principle often coincides with a compromised or corrupt relation to modernity, fundamentalism is almost always imbued with an anti-modernist rhetoric. The rhetoric, of course, conveniently obscures the fact that fundamentalism is always itself an innovation and an essentially post-modern one at that. Put in other terms, when it experiences that "the gods have abandoned the temple" of the (classic) religious tradition, fundamentalism sets out to build new altars of worship around its own fervour and conspicuous claims of identity as "the chosen." This is a post-modern strategy and, however, distasteful it can sometimes become, we ought to recognize its essentially, creative character.

As a radical, anti-modern (but still post-modern!) strategy, fundamentalism is prone to a variety of distortions — ranging from what can be called the neurotic, to the psychotic and indeed, as we have lately learned, the suicidal. But we are all aware that we can't explain the phenomenon from these extreme versions of it (although we may be able to do the reverse). Nor should we be taken in by fundamenalism's own rhetorical sleight of hand (i.e. in claiming to be simply a restoration and return to some pre-modern version of religion). If we look at two essential elements of fundamentalism, we see gestures which in themselves are authentic aspects of the human, religious enterprise. On the

16. Religious enclave that intentionally resists identification with the larger religious group in which it originally arose, on the basis that fundamental principles upon which the larger religious group is supposedly founded have become corrupt or displaced by alternative principles hostile to its identity.

one hand, there is the personally engaged posture of anti-modernity as it extends from Thoreau through Gandhi to Dorothy Day. No one could deny that this posture has been a profound source of creative renewal in the ethical, psychological and spiritual dimensions. On the other hand, there is the radical "identification of essential truths" against the grain of a settled religious tradition. This too has been a perennial activity of the great "transformers" of religious traditions (from Second Isaiah to Gautama, to Mahāvīra, to Jesus) and precisely as a critique of religiosity become sterile and oppressive.[17]

If these two essential elements of fundamentalism are "authentic" in themselves, then what may be said to be its distinguishing features are more defined by the emotional or psychological tone in which they are embodied: an anti-modernism that shades towards apocalyptic paranoia and a claim to possession of fundamental truth that reflects its "purity" outward as xenophobia and hatred of the other. This suggests that the critique of fundamentalism ought to derive from an ethic of moral and psychological development (rather than theology).[18] It also suggests then there is fundamentalism. If we are to understand, rather than simply demonize, I suggest again, that we consider the range of this moral and psychological spectrum. I picture a spectrum that stretches from the Amish farmer through the ultra-orthodox-Haredi and the member of Opus Dei to the Sinhala Buddhist of Sri Lanka to the teenage jihadist. Once again, I would argue, the primary shifts as one moves along this spectrum are not theological or religious as much as they are psychological and emotional. They are shifts of tone and intensity and ultimately,

---

17. Cf., Karen Armstrong, *The Great Transformation* (New York: Knopf, 2006).
18. In fact, we acknowledge this when we say, "Islam isn't about violence"; "Christianity isn't about excluding others," etc.

psychological maturity.

Another way to make the argument for this view clear would be to refer to the Dalai Lama. From one perspective, the Dalai Lama might be aptly considered "another example of Buddhist fundamentalism . . . [who] represents a vision of a feudal Tibetan state ruled by the clergy."[19] From another, he would be justly seen as one of the pioneers of contemporary spirituality, someone who successfully brought the Buddhist notion of compassion out of its historically narrow, pre-modern religious context into an exceptionally broad, post-modern public context. One might posit a similarly, enigmatic position for Jean Vanier whose undeniable fundamentalism was clearly always in vital balance with a very creative (post-modern), vision of spiritual poverty. In short, figures like these illustrate the middle range of what I would call a spectrum moving from fundamentalism through spirituality. Let me finally, then, focus on spirituality.

I have suggested that one historical source for what has come to be called spirituality is the development of the retreat centre itself as a locus of creative renewal in the Roman Catholic tradition. In that context, I have identified one central element of spirituality to be its *commitment to the open-ended and self-directed process of adult (self-) education — also by nature essentially creative and experimental.* Clearly, another historical and ongoing source of spirituality was and is the traditions of spiritualism, theosophy and the "new age" movements. These very eclectic and individualistic traditions always understood themselves to be essentially an "alternative" to dominant and dogmatic religious traditions as well as to an increasingly materialistic culture.[20] Because of this self-understanding, one

---

19. Benjamin Beit-Hallahmi, Fundamentalism, http://www.globalpolicy.org/wtc/fundamentalism/0501def.htm

20. Wikipedia, "New Age": "Most New Age practices and beliefs may be characterized as a form of alternative spirituality or →

finds a sourcing of movements considered "heretical" or "primitive" by dominant religions (from witchcraft through gnosticism to shamanism). These often also include marginalized mystical traditions (e.g. Kabbalah, esoteric Christianity, Sufism). Indeed, it is fair to say, I think, that this "alternativist" twist of new age spiritualism explains why it is perceived by many adherents of traditional religions as something "threatening" — along with a stridently relativist and antidogmatic attitude![21]

Still the condemnations — most notably the Vatican's *A Christian Reflection on the "New Age"* — are global in nature and, one must say, not very discriminating.[22] For example, cosmological spirituality — largely inspired by the great twentieth-century Catholic theologian Teilhard de Chardin

→ alternative religion. Even apparent exceptions, such as alternative medicine or traditional medicine practices, often have some spiritual dimension — such as a conceptual integration of mind, body, and spirit. The term New Age is generally limited to a Western or modern context where the Judeo-Christian tradition and/or Positivism are dominant, so the use of "alternative" in New Age thought generally implies a contrast with these dominant religious and/or scientific beliefs. Hence, many New Age ideas and practices contain either explicit or implied critiques of organized mainstream Christianity — emphasis on meditation suggests that simple prayer and faith is insufficient. Belief in reincarnation (which not all New Age followers accept) challenges familiar Christian doctrines of the afterlife."

21. Ibid., "New Age is syncretic in nature and has roots as a counter-cultural phenomenon. Thus New Age adherents tend to emphasize a relativist approach to truth, often referring to the Vedic statement of "one truth, but many paths," the mainstay of Hinduism, which idea is also found in the later Zen Buddhist spiritual dictum of "many paths, one mountain." This belief is not only an assertion of personal choice in spiritual matters, but also an assertion that truth itself is defined by the individual and his or her experience of it."

22. http://www.vatican.va/roman_curia/pontifical_councils/interelg/documents/rc_pc_interelg_doc_20030203_new-age_en.html#3.1.%20New%20Age%20as%20spirituality

— is hardly "new age" either historically or in substance. Neither, I think, are the profound and creative extensions of that vision into the context of deep ecology and global spirituality, most notably by the Passionist priest, Thomas Berry.[23] However, the condemnations also correctly identify the true nature of the shift into the post-modern world: for they themselves admit that what "corresponds to the legitimate spiritual longing of human nature" in this spirituality are (1) a new understanding of the universe (in a dynamic and wholistic, rather than static, mechanistic sense) and (2) a new understanding of the human person as both integrated into the universe and ultimately its creative agent.[24] By claiming that both of these positions "run counter to Christian revelation," the document is not only rejecting a scientific consensus (in quantum physics and other disciplines) but also the most deeply held convictions of post-modern spirituality.[25] Of course, it is true that this "cosmocentrism"

---

23. Ibid., ". . . the basic themes of esoteric culture are also present in the realms of politics, education and legislation. (p. 37) It is especially the case with ecology. Deep ecology's emphasis on bio-centrism denies the anthropological vision of the Bible, in which human beings are at the centre of the world, since they are considered to be qualitatively superior to other natural forms."

24. Ibid., "The move from a mechanistic model of classical physics to the "holistic" one of modern atomic and sub-atomic physics, based on the concept of matter as waves or energy rather than particles, is central to much New Age thinking"; ibid., "In what might be termed a classical New Age account, people are born with a divine spark, in a sense which is reminiscent of ancient gnosticism; this links them into the unity of the Whole. So they are seen as essentially divine, although they participate in this cosmic divinity at different levels of consciousness. We are co-creators, and we create our own reality."

25. Ibid. Even if it can be admitted that New Age religiosity in some way responds to the legitimate spiritual longing of human nature, it must be acknowledged that its attempts to do so run counter to Christian revelation.

and "personalism" can degenerate into an unthoughtful, esoteric pantheism, and a narrow, consumerist individualism respectively, but that is not their natural or best form. It is also clear that both principles emerged originally in the work of the Catholic theologian Teilhard de Chardin and there in an essentially Christian way. Moreover, while a whole subsequent generation of Catholic theologians have laboured to critically ground these two principles within the deepest traditions of Catholic Christianity — successfully, I would argue — they have also formed the basis for the broad Inter-religious consensus emerging between Christianity and Buddhism, Hinduism and Islam. In this sense, the principles may be said to correspond to deeply embedded elements of these religious traditions. Finally, one could also argue that they constitute the basis for a dialogue with scientific and humanist traditions.

If these two principles are at the core of contemporary spirituality, then a commitment to the open-ended process of adult (self-)education is its *modus operandi.* As we have noted this "implicates" spirituality in the problems of "relativism" and "experientialism" (as opposed to absolutism and dogmatism respectively). I use the word "implicates" here because I don't think all spirituality is simply relativist or experientialist. Rather I would suggest that here too, one can most appropriately speak of a spectrum along which various "spiritualities" find a balance between the uniquely, individual path of "growth" and the teachings/revelations of the great historical, social religious traditions. Let me also suggest that the criterion/distinction among these spiritualities has to do *with their dialogic relation, or openness to the wisdom of these great religious traditions*. So, for example, as I have just suggested, the cosmological spirituality developed by Teilhard de Chardin and broadened by a whole subsequent generation of theologians like Thomas Berry to encompass the new ecological perspectives of the post-modern world displays a critical, creative and broad-ranging dialogue with the Christian and other mystical and religious traditions (along with modern science). Precisely because of this, it embodies complex and critical interpretations of the principles of cosmocentrism and personalism. Contrast this version of spirituality for example with the one offered in the popular book by James Redfield, *The Celestine Prophecy.* The latter clearly displays a more casual and certainly less critical dialogue with the Christian and Gnostic traditions from which it draws its resources and for that reason embodies interpretations of cosmocentrism and personalism which are readily open to distortion (towards a facile utopianism and vague spiritism).

To return to the notion of the spectrum of spirituality — let me offer this very debatable but, I hope, suggestive example: from Redfield one could trace shades of gradually increasing, critical dialogue with religious traditions to Scientology, and thence to the "Dances of Universal Peace" developed by Samuel Lewis or towards the "integral spirituality" of Ken Wilber, further to the Shambhala teaching developed by Chogyam Trungpa and the Art of Living Foundation of Sri Sri Ravi Shankar, or still further, to the range of elaborate spiritualities associated with the work of Carl Jung and his followers and finally, to the work of Thomas Berry and Brian Swimme in *The New Universe Story.*

Naturally, this embodies a judgement of authenticity just as the range of fundamentalism embodied a judgement of emotional and psychological maturity. In both cases, however, the purpose is discrimination and therefore, also, an acceptance of the range of differences that exist among these post-modern strategies for religion. It strikes me that it is crucial for us, especially after 9/11 but also after the commercialization of religion in our generation, to acknowledge the "distortions" at both ends of the spectrum as part of the phenomenon of post-modern religion. To try to deny the religious element in violent fundamentalism or crassly materialistic spirituality — in order to protect some (imaginary) notion of pure religion ("That isn't true Islam," "That isn't true Christianity") — is just that, denial. "True" religion in the post-modern context is not some ideal form but, I think, that which would submit itself to a psychologically honest appraisal in order to come to fuller knowledge of itself. It is time, to that end, that religion owns up to its own shadows whether they are sexual abuse or violent hatred of others.

This brings me finally to the question of tolerance and its related question of identity-in-difference. I want to return to the "peculiar" place of the retreat centre to address it.

Identity and Tolerance in the Post-Modern World

I spoke of the post-modern context at the outset by using Jung's metaphor of the "temple abandoned by the gods." We might also say that post-modern human life is lived *extra ecclesiasm* and *extra naturam* (outside of the church and outside of nature).[26] Again, this has nothing to do with religious practice or membership but is primarily a function of the level of consciousness called "critical" or even "post-critical" — which has irrevocably lost the innocence necessary to live within a sacred temple or a sacred world. Those who are practising members of religious communities also function with this consciousness and, therefore, to one extent or another, must always first "willingly suspend their disbelief" in order to believe. The situation is different in the "peculiar" place of the retreat centre, however, because it exists consciously and explicitly in this desacralized, secular world — not as a pseudo-"temple" (or under the illusion that it could be!) but rather as

26. W. Giegerich, "Jung's Thought of the Self," in W. Giegerich, *The Neurosis of Psychology: Primary Papers towards a Critical Psychology*, (New Orleans: Spring Journal Books, 2005), 177: "This consciousness is *ipso facto extra naturam and extra ecclesiam. . . ."*

an open space in which the sacred is still sought but now in a radically new way, that is, by an engaged community following the path of spirituality through the *self-directed process of adult (self-)education*.

And so, the retreat centre is essentially a place of education rather than evangelization or proselytization, an open space or "sanctum" as sanctuary from which no one is excluded on the basis of their religious identity. Indeed, although it is rooted in a religious tradition and draws its values from it, its tolerance of difference is not defined by imposing a version of that traditional identity but rather by the commitment to the process of spirituality as self-education. The retreat centre may fail at this radical hospitality or tolerance and fall back on some absolutist or dogmatic criterion, but when it does so it has clearly failed.

Let me finally imagine how this notion of tolerance and identity could be applied conceptually to fundamentalism and spirituality in general.

The "commitment to an open-ended process of (self)-education" (spirituality) and "the identification of fundamental truths" (fundamentalism) seem incompatible principles and indeed, in practice, their collision is the source of constant conflict in many different realms of the post-modern world. If, as we have argued, the fundamentalist attempt "to identify with essential truths" is really an attempt to find and sustain religious identity in the post-modern context, then it really should be seen as *a struggle to develop and sustain psychological and emotional maturity without sacrificing the values of the spirit.* Moreover, this psychological and emotional maturity really means accepting the reality of the loss of religion (as it was) and maintaining an openness to religion as it may be.[27] As we

27. Giegerich, Rupture, 230 "As long as we cling to our religions, we blind ourselves to the divine that would show itself in utterly

→

are well aware the struggle in which fundamentalism is engaged can be a violent and deadly one, but we may also become aware that a great deal is at stake in it — also for all of us. By the same token, spirituality may be seen as *a struggle to sustain the vision of a possibility of spiritual life in a materialistic and debased (self-indulgent) culture.* This also has to do with accepting the loss of religion as it was (dogmatic and absolutist) and taking up the task of religion as it may become — namely, as a spiritual quest that is essentially open-ended. This means taking up the project of religious identity again in a new way as a project of self-education. That, I think, is the true basis of tolerance. And it has to do with recovering an insight buried in all the great religious traditions: *Is it not the empty hand, and the empty hand alone, that can be filled?*[28]

→ new and unimagined shape from within our real world. We would monotonously repeat the same old answer, even after a new question has been asked."

28. Ibid., 231.

3

Interfaith Friendship : A Bridge to Peace

Susan Kennel Harrison

I WANT to share with you my conviction that the world needs more interfaith friendships if it wants to have sustainable cultures of peace. This conviction is rooted in a religiously based commitment to the goal of peace between all people; a peace that is not only characterized by the absence of violence but also by the presence of justice and dignity for all persons. My conviction, that we need more interfaith friendships, is also based in a praxis, a lived experience of peace-making through understanding, which has come about primarily through the medium of friendship. So, I want to first explain what I mean by friendship, particularly across faith communities, and then I want to describe the story of a particular experience of interfaith friendship.

Friendship, when successful, involves bridging the I and thou[1] gap with a bridge that can be freely travelled back and forth across. Friendship implies more than an acquaintance, it implies an ongoing relationship with another person; a relationship that is actively nurtured and sustained. What sustains a friendship, what keeps it going, can vary greatly,

1. Martin Buber, *I and Thou* (New York: Charles Scribner's Sons, 1958).

as we shall explore later, but the fact that it is a sustained relationship is a very important detail, and significant to why interfaith friendship can be a bridge to peace.

Sometimes friendships come about by accident, at least we cannot humanly discern why or when the relationship began and took root. But, the kind of friendship I am referring to, is the kind that represents intentional acts of meeting, sharing, listening, and responding to another person, as an-*other*. A good friendship is characterized by being accepted as one is. This isn't to say one will not be challenged to mature, grow, and even change. But a friend does not make those changes a prerequisite to their relationship to the other; does not require the other to earn the relationship in some way. Yet a friendship often inspires one to consider changes because the nature of one's self-understanding is expanded in the context of the relationship. Often we come to understand and know ourselves more carefully as a result of relationship with someone who is *other* than us. In a good friendship, our sum becomes more than who we are as two separate individuals.

A good friendship is characterized by two-way communication. While this communication can involve provocation and conflicts, it is not primarily characterized in this way. Rather, the communication involves a give and take of questions and vulnerable sharing that allows for self-disclosure, explanation, clarification, wonder, joy, humour, as well as comfort and the sharing of pain and confusion. The ultimate outcome in the process of friendship involves mutual understanding and a process of journeying in life together, towards something that extends beyond ourselves. Friendship between people of faith also involves the element of building up one another as religious practitioners, through example and through respect of each other's faith journeys. With time a good friendship sharpens us, clarifies our choices, including the practice and understanding of our religious practice and faith.

Because of these characteristics in friendship, it strikes me as odd when we write and speak of interreligious *dialogue* then describe a process that is commonly characterized by religious leaders, often men, sitting around a conference table and talking *at* one another about what they believe. What is meant by "dialogue" is a typically formal procedure of exchanging information through journals and orchestrated situations. But less often recognized is what some catholic writers have called "the dialogue of life."[2] That is, the kind of natural sharing of information and experiences with others that occurs in the everyday ebb and flow of living nearby and being conscious of one another. Too often we assume that multi-culturalism, like that of Canada, will automatically create this dialogue of life, but this is not necessarily so. People will gravitate to those who share their religious outlook, their language and culture. As someone put it earlier this week, we become a culture of tolerance, which means co-existing. Co-existence is not the same as befriending. So interfaith friendship, and the dialogue of life, needs to be something intentionally cultivated and sustained in our societies. But such relationships, like those between people of different faiths, often mean crossing between cultures, religious language and symbols, in addition to the risky business of reaching out towards a stranger in friendship. Given this reality, that of the risk taking involved in creating friendships, I want to tell the story of an experiment in friendship creating that I have been a part of since 1998.

This story begins in 1990 when there was a terrible earthquake in northern Iran. At this time, the Mennonite Central Committee (MCC), a service and relief organization of the Mennonite church, "wanted to respond to the disaster

---

2. Dialogue of life, dialogue of humanitarian action, dialogue of theological exchange, dialogue of spiritual experience.

because of the magnitude of human suffering and to demonstrate our commitment to provide assistance to people in need "without racial, gender, religious, or political qualification."[3] Because the state of relations between the governments of the United States, where MCC headquarters is located, and the Islamic Republic of Iran, MCC "considered it important to try to promote friendship and understanding between the people of Iran and North America."

In the context of working with the Iranian Red Crescent Society on the long-term reconstruction after the earthquake, "a four person MCC delegation visited Iran in early January 1991."[4] The director general for international affairs in Iran at that time was Mr Sadreddin Sadr.

> Mr Sadr had a vision for how the collaboration of MCC, a Christian humanitarian agency from Canada and the United States, and the Iranian Red Crescent Society, an essentially Muslim organization from Iran, could contribute to building bridges of friendship and understanding between the people of Iran and North America, in addition to serving the needs of refugees and victims of disasters.[5]

A student exchange programme was proposed in order to promote more interaction between North American Mennonites and Iranians. Dr Ed Martin, of MCC, contacted Dr Seyed Kazem Sajjadpour, who was working at Iran's permanent mission to the United Nations in New York at the time. Dr Sajjadpour arranged for Dr Martin to meet with the then ambassador Dr Kamal Kahrazzi, and the two of them lent their support to the proposal for a student exchange by taking it to Iran. Much to MCC's surprise it was the Imam

3. Ed Martin, "MCC and Iran," *Mennonite Central Committee Peace Office Publications*, July-September 2001; Vol. 31, no. 3, p. 1.
4. Ibid., p. 2.
5. Ibid.

Khomeini Education and Research Institute (IKERI) in Qom, Iran which responded favourably to the idea of a student exchange.[6]

A student exchange programme was organized after some negotiations which allowed for students from the Institute in Iran to study in seminaries or universities in Canada, while MCC could send students to study at the Institute in Qom. The first Mennonites, perhaps the first Christians ever to live there, went in 1998 to live in Qom, a city of scholars and clerics. This couple studied Farsi and Islam and attended class while also participating in a class on Christianity, taught at the Institute for the Muslim seminarians.

In the same year the Institute sent two of their best graduate students to come and live in Toronto and study Philosophy of Religion. In Toronto, they are the only Muslims registered at the Toronto School of Theology, and were initially hosted by the Toronto Mennonite Theological Centre (TMTC). Since the inception of the exchange two other Mennonite Christian couples have moved to Qom, and several of the Institute's scholars have come to meet with us in Toronto, as well as at the Conrad Grebel University college in Waterloo, Ontario, staying for varying amounts of time.

The professors of the institutions involved have come to know one another and as a result of the student exchange developed their own academic dialogue, which has resulted in an ongoing biannual academic conference between the Mennonite scholars and scholars from Qom. In a recent article discussing these academic conferences Professor A. James Reimer, a Mennonite theologian involved in these academic conferences, wrote —

> Apparent throughout our discussions was an increasing level of trust between our two communities of learning.

6. Ibid.

> Pivotal to this trust is the sincerity of the dialogue, the common search for truth, and the firm conviction that the life of the intellect must not be separated from devotion, piety and moral integrity.[7]

More about those academic conferences can be read of in the fall 2003 and winter 2006 issues of *The Conrad Grebel Review*. There is much I could say about these academic conferences, but for our purposes today, I want to adhere to a description and evaluation of the "dialogue of life" aspect of this exchange.

I have had the privilege of coordinating the Toronto side of this exchange since the beginning of this exchange and have learned *many many* things about these friends from Iran, their religion, their country, their culture, as well as learning to see my own community, faith, and country through their eyes. The students who came from Qom have also been transformed through this experience. To quote Mr Daneshvar:

> . . . now I believe more strongly than I did at any time before that humanity today desperately needs the help of religions to overcome the ever-growing predicaments on the globe. I can hardly imagine that religions can provide this help without conducting a serious and friendly dialogue between themselves. . . .[8]

With this background, let me discuss some of the various venues we've tried to create "first dates" between our communities, and I will discuss some of the specific barriers we've become aware of thus far. Most importantly though, I want to emphasize the notion of *sustained* relationship, which I have come to believe is the singular most important way this kind of relationship can bridge peace in societies. As David

---

7. James Reimer, "Shi'ah Muslim — Mennonite Christian Dialogue II: Introduction," *The Conrad Grebel Review*, Winter 2006: p. 6.
8. Ibid., p. 12.

Ford[9] stated, diplomatic and politically structured peace agreements cannot create peace, but the work of building relationships can create and *sustain* a culture of peace, once the diplomatic solutions are able to be drafted and implemented. Without the grass roots work of friendship and community building between the various religious communities in our societies, no amount of diplomacy or legislation can provide the soil in which such seeds of peace and diplomatic agreements can take root and flourish. I will add that as long as countries label each other as enemies — one on one friendships are the most effective way of discovering that the so-called enemy has a face, and to learn the nature of the injustices that are felt between those nations. Interfaith friendships allow us to hear the news media differently, and give us a basis for caring about peace, beyond our own interests of peace in the world.

My role with the Iranian exchange students was initially focused on helping them and their families settle into Canada, adjust to student life at Toronto School of Theology, and to learn English. As they became settled, we began to spend more of our time visiting one another and talking about our religious beliefs. We each came readily to see that we often expected each other to be the spokesperson for the *whole* of our faith. This has also become evident when my Muslim friends are invited to talk about their beliefs for church groups. This "use" of each other in speaking engagements has become a source of humour, so that whenever a Mennonite group requests the presence of one of the Muslim guests to explain Islam to their group, I typically tell my friends, in jest, that their presence is requested at such and such church, so that they can single-handedly represent and explain the whole of

9. Professor David Ford, Regius Professor of Divinity, and Fellow of Selwyn College, University of Cambridge.

Islam. My friends have found the role daunting, to say the least. They want to provide compelling arguments for their religious beliefs, but they do not want to have to itemize all the varieties within Islam. More problematic however, has been the misinformation and ignorance that they have encountered among their Christian audiences. This is not only troubling but also frustrating because of the need to continually engage in conversation on a very basic explanatory level about Islam, foregoing the possibility of a more productive nuanced conversation. Interfaith Friendship on the reverse side, the Mennonite Christians living in Iran also find themselves in a position of explaining the basic points of Christian belief, and are humbled by the knowledge that they represent a small minority within a large and diverse Christian tradition. Both sides, however, have valued the opportunity to explain their faith first-hand, rather than their audiences learning what Christianity is about from a Muslim teacher, or vice versa. Of course, the largest challenge when teaching about someone else's religion is to do it in such a way that they recognize themselves in your description of them! Whenever possible, we share with each other what we are going to write or say about the other, to receive feedback and clarification regarding where we may still misunderstand the other.

I am convinced that face to face meetings are the best ways to cure people of their stereotypes of one another, a praxis I recently learned is called "contact theory."[10] Because I am committed to the notion that if people are brought together, and moved out of their comfort zones, they will experience *the other* in ways that influence their thinking and challenge their stereotypes, I have worked hard at trying to find various venues in which the Muslim students could meet members of

10. Deborah L. Plummer, *Racing Across the Lines: Changing Race Relations through Friendship* (Cleveland: Pilgrim Press, 2004), p. 56.

the Ontario Mennonite community, and beyond. We tried book study groups for several years. The Muslim guests came to monthly student meetings sponsored by the Toronto Mennonite theological centre. We met with the Graduate Christian student fellowship group on the University of Toronto campus; spoke in adult Sunday school classes; modelled interfaith dialogue from the pulpit and at the annual meeting of Canadian Mennonites, we even tried a joint fishing excursion. The hope was that by creating venues by which good "first dates" could take place, participants would feel comfortable initiating further relationship with our Muslim guests. Typically, Mennonites are known for hospitality, particularly around food, so I was surprised when further interactions were not taking place. The experience has led us to observe that the only really successful dialogical encounters have taken place *in the contexts of friendships;* that is relationships that have an overarching binding commitment.

So what circumstances have lent themselves to this kind of friendship? Initially MCC thought that by bringing the Muslim students to Toronto School of Theology friendships would naturally spring up through classroom encounters and *vis-à-vis* the Mennonite student gatherings. But this was not the case. The friendships developed in the context of other frameworks that required ongoing contact and co-operation between Mennonites and the Muslim guests. In one case, the relationship began as English conversation practice between two philosophy students, one Muslim and the other Mennonite. There was a weekly commitment to meet and talk together in English to facilitate language acquisition, which consequently had a shared academic focus as well. The two participants did not, and continue not to have very much in common in terms of their convictions and academic positions, but the overall commitment was to meet weekly, a commitment that was sustained for as many as five years. Neither participant succeeded in converting the other, religiously, nor academically, but a trust and camaraderie was built *vis-à-vis* the commitment to be in relationship. Each came to clearly understand the other's beliefs, piety, and academic approach, and could sharpen one another by their vast differences. More importantly, each learned how to relate in a sustained fashion to someone who held opposing convictions. The ability to provoke, challenge and confront, while staying in relationship, was sustained by the primary commitment to be in relationship with one another for the sake of learning about the other, as an other. Thus, it was a relationship that was neither comfortable, nor easy, but rewarding and authentic nonetheless.

What we also observed was that in a highly diverse setting such as Toronto University housing, Mennonites looked for others like themselves, and the Muslims likewise looked for other Iranian families to relate to. This is consistent with notions of identity reinforcement. In many cases, the Muslim family life was at a different stage than similarly aged Mennonite students, which led to a difference in interests and needs in daily life interactions. The wives of Mennonites were typically reluctant to get involved because of the more visible difference of the practice of Muslim women, wearing the modest clothes covering called *hijab*. Many Mennonite women, of the Swiss Brethren and Amish ancestry, have come from a recent history of wearing a uniform dress code,[11] a practice widely rejected in certain circles of Mennonites, typically

---

11. The uniform dress code has a variety of modest dress for women, everything from long black skirts and bonnets that completely cover their hair, to a modest dress with floral print and bobby socks, or skin coloured nylons. Men's attire would include omitting a tie (the same for Iranians, but as a protest of Western dress infiltration), and not wearing a suit with a lapel. The more conservative dress code can go so far as to omit the use of zippers as well.

among those in higher educational situations. Thus while this experience in recent Mennonite history could provide a natural bridge for their women to understand this dress choice among Muslim women, more often it became a cause for rejection of those women who choose to practice *hijab* in a Western context, where it is not required of them. As many Westerners, Mennonite women presume that a Muslim woman wears *hijab* for reasons other than her personal choice of piety, forgetting that our own mothers and grandmothers wore coverings and plain dress because they personally believed 1 Cor. 11, where it stated that this practice would serve to keep them right with God — a position they wholeheartedly desired as committed Christians. Despite our history, it is hard to imagine that a Muslim woman chooses to wear *hijab* out of her conviction that this practice facilitates her ability to be in right relationship with God, something I have come to see as foremost in many Muslim women's hearts and minds. I continue to wrestle with the barrier of the public face of Islam, as expressed in the dress of religious women. In many ways, these Muslim women would have so much they share in common with the more conservative Mennonite women, regarding the day-to-day way they live out their sincerity in following God in all aspects of life; a shared morality and priority of prayer, scripture study, commitment to participation in community, simple living, avoidance of ostentatiousness, care of those in need, desire to seek edifying leisure activities, and cautiousness about involvement in broader society, and so on.

MCC also anticipated that children would bring Mennonite and Muslim families together, as so often children do serve this vital community building function. But this also proved not to be the case. In some ways the different expectations around manners, be they cultural or religiously informed, played a significant role. Language barriers at times contributed to breakdown of this opportunity, but overall families of the two groups did not interact frequently enough for the children to form the kinds of bonds that kept their families interacting with one another.

I observed that Mennonite and Muslim families utilized their leisure time differently. For example, while both groups watched TV in their leisure, the Muslim families early on found Western programming unacceptable, and limited their TV use to satellite channels from Iran. So, a common parlance around TV shows was not available as a bridge for friendship building. Having said that, in my own relationship with the Muslim families, I have valued the opportunities to watch television shows from their home country with them. Technology allows that they could watch in Farsi language while I have access to simultaneous English subtitles, allowing us to talk about the shows, and laugh at the punchlines together. Watching popular TV shows from Iran became invaluable to me in learning to understand what themes in life are of foremost importance to my friends from Iran. I observed that family honour, marriage arrangements and marriage relations, as well as death, and civic life, are frequently the source of TV programming. I also observed that between programming there was often meditative traditional music and scenes from around the country, as well as Qur'anic teaching. As someone highly skeptical of government censoring TV programming, I came to appreciate the commercial free nature of TV programming. Conversely, my Muslim friends came to find the constant bombardment of ads, forbidden images and suggestive themes, found in the majority of our media productions, and marketing, as too destructive to justify having Western TV programming available in their homes; they did not want their lives, nor that of their children, exposed to unedifying images and thoughts any time the programming was turned on. As a Mennonite I also struggle with this reality, and share their values, but I have not yet made the decision to refuse to have a TV in my home.

A particularly meaningful part of our friendship building has been in the ongoing shared comparison of global stories between our country's media. For example, on the day that Saddam Hussein's statues were being pulled down, I watched CNN coverage while my friends watched Hezbollah news coverage. While watching our TV news simultaneously, we spoke on the phone and reported to one another what each of our newscasters were saying about the same event. It was a day that my eyes were opened tremendously to the vastly different ways that the same momentous event could be interpreted in the media. Since this time I have made a conscious effort to scan Canadian news about Iran, and when I find it, I try to read or discuss the reports directly with the Iranian exchange students. Typically, I learn how the news story failed to capture the nuanced nature of the particular event or person they were covering. An example was an article in *The Globe and Mail* several weeks ago, in which it was stated that, in October 2005, President Ahmadinijad of Iran banned all Western music on radio and TV and public venues. While the newspaper article admitted that few Iranians are respecting the ban, it unequivocally made the point that the new President was anti-Western in yet another extreme way.[12] I got on the phone and called my Iranian friends to ask if this ban was indeed in place. They were as surprised as I was to hear of it. They drew my attention, as did the newspaper, to the reality that Western music is regularly listened to in Iran, even played by the Symphony Orchestra of Tehran. While *The Globe and Mail* wrote a story that framed Iran and its new president as moving "backwards" in its value of the things so important in

12. "Western music banned on Iranian state TV, radio" 20/12/05, *The Globe and Mail*, p. A20.

the West, it did so in a way that even Iranians did not recognize their own country in the newspaper coverage. Thus, a tremendous value of interfaith friendships consists of having a place to "test the news," often getting a more nuanced picture of the story being covered. Comparative news conversation, then, is a productive way of interacting and building interfaith friendship. It provides a venue for asking clarifying questions, thereby inviting the other person to share of themselves, their experiences, observations, disappointments, and hopes. In addition, it facilitates the creation of empathy; the ability to hear the news through the ears and eyes of the other, an ability that is sorely needed in our times. Comparative news sharing provides a venue for discovering what really matters to one another, and equips persons to safeguard the pride and dignity of each other more compassionately. Most importantly, it does not need a specialist to happen, for anyone can talk and listen to their friend about the news!

We also observed that husbands and wives of Mennonite families typically invite others, *as couples*, to their homes, to share a meal and share socially together in a relaxed fashion. This did not happen frequently between the Mennonite and Muslim families, in part because of the experience of the women Muslim guests not feeling comfortable to talk openly in co-ed gatherings around a table, as well as the intimidation felt by Mennonite hosts around the issues of providing acceptable *halāl* meals; *halāl* meals were a cause of anxiety for these visiting Muslims as well, because they do not accept all foods that bear the label *halāl*. In one case I was told about a Mennonite family, which had invited the Shi'ite guests to their home for a meal. When the meal was served, the Muslim guest pulled his own sandwich from his briefcase to eat at their table. In another case, the Muslim family brought their own food and cooked it at the home of the Mennonite family, and the two families ate together, sharing one another's food. More commonly, Mennonites who acted as host found that food ordered from a restaurant which the Muslim guests stated was acceptable to eat, or serving a vegetarian meal caused the least problems.

Because food is such an important part of both Shi'ite and Mennonite cultures, and their ways of being together within their religious communities, this has proven to be a significant barrier, and has left the Mennonite community feeling inhibited to know of other ways of welcoming the Muslims to their homes. In turn, Muslims have their own religious obligations around hospitality and not offending their hosts, which create anxiety and discomfort for them in mixed faith and co-ed situations involving food.

Of course, in reality, this barrier is not as difficult as it appears, but because of the stereotypes on both sides, it has not been easy to find Mennonites willing to risk inviting the Muslim guests, and adjust their cooking and food purchasing around the dietary laws of their guests. It is my belief that if Mennonites could get to know these Muslim families a little bit more in some comfortable venue, they would be able to learn, as friends, about the dietary restrictions and find creative ways to work together at meeting one another around meals. So, again, despite my conviction that interfaith friendships are the hope for creating societies that can nurture and sustain a culture of peace, the *manner in which those friendships can be started* is a challenge I am still working on.

I have tried in more recent years to pay more attention to the comfort zone of Muslim women, who prefer to be in an all women social setting. In this manner I have hosted "ladies night out" in which Muslim and Christian women have gathered at homes to socialize, watch movies, listen to guest speakers, among other things. Most recently, several of us Muslim and Mennonite women embarked on a two-day camping trip together. The dietary laws were less of a problem than the challenge to keep our socializing in English, so that everyone could feel included in the conversation, and the observation that we enjoyed nature at a different pace. But in addition to our own experience of coming closer to one another through this shared experience, which involved lots of humour and co-operation, I noticed that those who camped nearby us were also watching us with interest. Some of our campsite neighbours made attempts to reach out and visit with us, and I realized that *the act of being seen together* as Muslims and Mennonites was probably a significant mediation for other peoples' ability to consider the possibilities of this kind of obvious interfaith friendship.

While we have experimented with a wide variety of ways to bring the Mennonites and Muslims together, the only ongoing relationships have been sustained by *a commitment to friendship*. In such a context we have become human beings together — people who care about living rightly before God — which includes reaching out to those who some nations are telling us not to trust. It has been in the regular conversations and sharing between us in the dialogue of life that we have learned about one another, what shapes our anxieties and faith, and we are brought together in deepening commitments to each other.

We learned about funerals and marriage ceremonies[13] of each other's religions because as friends we talked, cried, and celebrated when relatives died, married or had a new baby. We have not learned about the holy days of each other's religion from book learning, but rather from the "dialogue of life." We would happen to call or visit at times when we were preparing for religious ceremonies and the meaning of those

13. We are still waiting for a Western/Mennonite wedding invitation to be extended to our guests, for the sake of their observation and learning, if for no other reasons.

ceremonies became known to us through the friendship. Because of the sustained nature of the friendship relationship, we can talk about our misunderstandings and disappointments as well, in a manner of respect, trust and commitment to see the relationship through the tough times.

I take comfort that when my friends return to Iran and begin teaching other Muslims about what Christians believe, they will also say that Christians in America and Canada are not all the same — that the loud voices of the Western politicians are not the only voices in the West. And when Westerners glibly bash Iranian women or the Mullahs I can confidently offer another perspective — that of the human face of my friends from Qom. These are the relationships that can advocate confidently for peace — and if and when diplomacy ever makes peace possible, there will be a fabric of relationship already in place to sustain it. This is why I believe that interfaith friendships are a bridge to a lasting sustainable peace.

4

A Bahá'í Perspective on Human Rights and the World's Religions After September 11

Brian D. Lepard

IN this presentation my aim is to explore and articulate a Bahá'í perspective on human rights and the world's religions after the atrocious terrorist attacks of 11 September 2001, not to mention more recent terrorist bombings. This paper contains my own views and not those of any Bahá'í institution. I will first briefly investigate the Bahá'í view of human rights as God-given rights that are inalienable by any human agency and that apply to all human beings without distinctions based on race, religion, or nationality. I will also examine Bahá'í teachings on the unity of religions and the imperative of eradicating religious prejudice, which lies at the root of the attacks of 11 September. I will then outline some of the social reforms that are necessary, in the Bahá'í view, to safeguard universal respect for human rights. Finally, in the light of this framework, I will comment on the draft Universal Declaration of Human Rights by the World's Religions and suggest various additional points that might be made in this groundbreaking document.

Human Rights as God-Given Rights

In the Bahá'í perspective, the term "human rights" properly refers to rights that are enjoyed by all human beings, without exception, by virtue of their quality of being human. But the source of those rights is not human society itself; rather human rights are conferred on human beings by an All-Loving God. And these rights derive in turn from our spiritual dignity resulting from our potential to enter into a relationship with God. In this connection, the Prophet-Founder of the Bahá'í Faith, Bahá'u'lláh, has proclaimed that human beings alone among God's creatures uniquely possess the capacity to know and love God, a capacity itself that results from God's love for humanity. Bahá'u'lláh affirms, speaking with the voice of God, "O Son of Being! Love Me, that I may love thee. If thou lovest Me not, My love can in no wise reach thee. Know this, O Servant."[1]

In the light of this spiritual reality of humanity, it is shameful that human rights violations are so omnipresent around the world. Day by day thousands, if not hundreds of thousands, of human beings become the victims of starvation, torture, rape, or murder, while their oppressors are often never brought to justice.

Bahá'u'lláh declares that the time has come to bring about universal respect for human rights. He announces that this purpose is to establish justice for all people, and to eliminate tyranny. He advises the world's leaders:

> God hath committed into your hands the reins of the government of the people, that ye may rule with justice over them, safeguard the rights of the downtrodden, and punish the wrong-doers.[2]

Human Rights and the Global Human Family

In the Bahá'í view, human rights not only have a spiritual foundation, grounded in the inherent nobility of every human

1. Bahá'u'lláh, *The Hidden Words* (Arabic), tr. Shoghi Effendi (Wilmette, Ill.: Bahá'í Publishing Trust, 2003), no. 5.
2. Bahá'u'lláh, *Gleanings from the Writings of Bahá'u'lláh*, 2nd rev. edn., tr. Shoghi Effendi (Wilmette, Ill.: Bahá'í Publishing Trust, 1976), p. 247.

being as a creation of God. They also are a manifestation of the unity of the global human family, a unity that has always been a spiritual reality but that can now be actualized through world-encompassing societal transformation, a transformation that is God's will for this age in human history. Bahá'u'lláh teaches that we are living in a time in which world unity is no longer a pious and fuzzy ideal in the minds of radical philosophers or far-sighted visionaries, but a social imperative. The realization of increasing levels of unity and co-operation among all constituent members of the global human family permits a far-reaching evolution in our conception and implementation of human rights. At the same time, working to promote universal human rights is a precondition for achieving a more harmonious and peaceful global civilization.

Thus, Bahá'u'lláh declares, "The well-being of mankind, its peace and security, are unattainable unless and until its unity is firmly established."[3] Indeed, Bahá'u'lláh says that throughout history humanity's spiritual evolution has been manifested socially by a progression in stages of social unity, from the family, to the tribe, and to the nation. Today, He announces, all humanity is one, and indeed, is spiritually one nation. In this regard, He affirms: "The earth is but one country, and mankind its citizens."[4]

This teaching means that human rights are not merely claims that each individual has against society, or against others, to be exercised as if that individual were an end unto himself. Rather, human rights are linked intimately with our identity as members of a unified family, in which each individual has duties to promote the welfare of his or her family, community, nation, and the whole of the human race, and yet is entitled to reciprocal rights and respect within each

3. Ibid., p. 286.
4. Ibid., p. 250.

of these levels of social unity and co-operation. And it means that human rights are not merely the concern of governments, or the state, or the police; rather, every one of us has solemn and inalienable responsibilities to respect the rights and promote the spiritual and material welfare of every other member of our global human family.

This conception allows us to move from the traditional secular adversarial conception of rights, in which the state is viewed as a potential rival of the individual, and the individual demands rights from the state, towards a more holistic notion. This holistic perspective sees individuals and their states and communities as elements of a global partnership aimed at improving the well-being of all mankind.

A Dynamic Conception of Equality, Including Equality of the Races and of the Sexes

Bahá'u'lláh's teachings of the divine character and purpose of human beings, as well as the reality of the solidarity of the human family as one spiritual community, point towards a dynamic conception of human equality, a conception in which each human being, of whatever race, sex, nationality or religion, is regarded as a repository of spiritual potentialities, a mirror that can reflect divine virtues towards others. Because each of us has this potential and capacity, we are fundamentally equal, and Bahá'u'lláh's laws thus prohibit categorically any discrimination based on race, sex, ethnicity or any other factor that is irrelevant to our divinely-appointed mission. He also urges us to purge from our hearts every form of prejudice, for we are all equally humble creatures of God. Speaking as the mouthpiece of God, He writes:

> O Children of Men! Know ye not why We created you all from the same dust? That no one should exalt himself over the other. Ponder at all times in your hearts how ye were created. Since We have created you all from one same

> substance it is incumbent on you to be even as one soul, to walk with the same feet, eat with the same mouth and dwell in the same land, that from your inmost being, by your deeds and actions, the signs of oneness and the essence of detachment may be made manifest.[5]

Bahá'u'lláh, in His laws, swept away outdated prejudices and practices, including those based on religion, that subjugated one group to another. In the words of 'Abdu'l-Bahá, the eldest son of Bahá'u'lláh and the authorized interpreter of His teachings, Bahá'u'lláh taught that "prince, peer and peasant alike have equal rights to just treatment."[6]

More specifically, the Bahá'í teachings put an end to the institution of slavery and millennia of discrimina0tion against dark-skinned peoples. Bahá'u'lláh pronounces in his Book of Laws: "Let no man exalt himself above another; all are but bondslaves before the Lord, and all exemplify the truth that there is none other God but Him."[7] Bahá'u'lláh specifically outlawed any discrimination or prejudice based on race. He announces: "Close your eyes to racial differences, and welcome all with the light of oneness."[8]

In a speech at Howard University in Washington, D.C. in 1912, 'Abdu'l-Bahá stated:

> There are no whites and blacks before God. All colors are one, and that is the color of servitude to God. . . . Strive

---

5. Bahá'u'lláh, *The Hidden Words* (Arabic), no. 68.
6. 'Abdu'l-Bahá, *Paris Talks: Addresses Given by 'Abdu'l-Bahá in Paris in 1911-1912* (New Delhi: Bahá'í Publishing Trust, 1971), p. 154.
7. Bahá'u'lláh, *The Kitáb-i-Aqdas: The Most Holy Book* (Haifa: Bahá'í World Centre, 1992), p. 45, K72.
8. Quoted in Shoghi Effendi, *The Advent of Divine Justice* (Wilmette, Ill.: Bahá'í Publishing Trust, 1966), p. 31.

> jointly to make extraordinary progress and mix together completely.[9]

On the subject of racial prejudice, 'Abdu'l-Bahá declares:

> Concerning the prejudice of race: it is an illusion, a superstition pure and simple! For God created us all of one race. There were no differences in the beginning, for we are all descendants of Adam. . . . In the sight of God there is no difference between the various races. Why should man invent such a prejudice? How can we uphold war caused by an illusion?[10]

Bahá'u'lláh also asserted the complete moral indefensibility of doctrines promoting the inherent superiority of men over women. Bahá'u'lláh declares: "Women and men have been and always will be equal in the sight of God."[11] He further affirms that today women must attain social equality with men, and all forms of discrimination against women must be eliminated. Furthermore, Bahá'u'lláh proclaimed that preference should be given to educating women over men.

'Abdu'l-Bahá explained these teachings of Bahá'u'lláh, stating that historically women have been treated as ignorant and relegated to the home. "Bahá'u'lláh destroyed these ideas," he says, "and proclaimed the equality of man and woman. He made woman respected by commanding that all women be educated, that there be no difference in the education of the two sexes and that man and woman share the same rights. In

---

9. 'Abdu'l-Bahá, *The Promulgation of Universal Peace: Talks Delivered by 'Abdu'l-Bahá During His Visit to the United States and Canada in 1912*, 2nd edn., comp. Howard MacNutt (Wilmette, Ill.: Bahá'í Publishing Trust, 1982), pp. 44-46.
10. 'Abdu'l-Bahá, *Paris Talks*, p. 148.
11. Bahá'u'lláh, in *The Compilation of Compilations Prepared by the Universal House of Justice, 1963-1990* (Maryborough, Victoria: Bahá'í Publications Australia, 1991), vol. 2, p. 379.

the estimation of God there is no distinction of sex."[12] He asserts that when, the equality of the sexes is realized thanks to the education of women, war will cease because women will not allow it.[13]

The Unity of Religions and the Scourge of Religious Prejudice

Of particular relevance to the theme of this conference, Bahá'u'lláh proclaimed that all the world's great religions are founded on authentic and equally valid Revelations from a single God, Revelations carried by divinely-appointed Prophets, or Manifestations, who are incomparable in their spiritual purity and peerless among human beings. These Manifestations, He taught, are like mirrors that reflect the brilliant light of the Divine to a humanity sorely in need of spiritual enlightenment. These Manifestations include Kṛṣṇa, the Buddha, Zoroaster, Abraham, Moses, Christ, Muhammad, and in our days, the Báb and Bahá'u'lláh, the twin prophets of the Bahá'í Faith. Bahá'u'lláh further taught that all of these Manifestations have shared with humanity a timeless message of love and reconciliation, while also bringing particular social laws and principles adapted to the stage of civilization in which each appeared.

Bahá'u'lláh exhorts us to love those of other faiths, not only because they are fellow members of the human family, but because all the great world religions together represent one unfolding Revelation from one God, a Revelation whose purpose is to bring about unity and love among all human beings. He teaches: "Consort with the followers of all religions in a spirit of friendliness and fellowship."[14] He forbids religious

---

12. 'Abdu'l-Bahá, *The Promulgation of Universal Peace*, p. 166.
13. Ibid., p. 175.
14. Bahá'u'lláh, *Tablets of Bahá'u'lláh Revealed after the Kitáb-i-Aqdas*, tr. Habib Taherzadeh (Haifa: Bahá'í World Centre, 1978), p. 22.

fanaticism, prejudice, and conflict, warning us that religious "fanaticism and hatred are a world-devouring fire, whose violence none can quench."[15] Bahá'u'lláh instead reminds us that the "purpose of religion as revealed from the heaven of God's holy Will is to establish unity and concord amongst the peoples of the world; make it not the cause of dissension and strife."[16] 'Abdu'l-Bahá explains that Bahá'u'lláh taught that "religion must be the source of unity and fellowship in the world. If it is productive of enmity, hatred and bigotry, the absence of religion would be preferable."[17]

Because all religions have counselled us to love one another, 'Abdu'l-Bahá says that "religious prejudice is especially opposed to the will and command of God."[18] Religious prejudice is based instead on blind adherence to dogmas that separate religions from one another. 'Abdu'l-Bahá explains,

> The strife between religions, nations and races arises from misunderstanding. If we investigate the religions to discover the principles underlying their foundations, we will find they agree; for the fundamental reality of them is one and not multiple. By this means the religionists of the world will reach their point of unity and reconciliation.[19]

Lamentably, religious prejudice and fanaticism appear to be ascendant, a development that the Universal House of Justice, the international governing body of the Bahá'í Faith asserted, in an April 2002 statement to the religious leaders of the world, should be viewed with alarm. It declared in that statement: "The greater part of organized religion stands paralyzed at

---

15. Bahá'u'lláh, *Gleanings*, p. 288.
16. Bahá'u'lláh, *Tablets of Bahá'u'lláh*, p. 129.
17. 'Abdu'l-Bahá, *The Promulgation of Universal Peace*, p. 434.
18. Ibid., p. 316.
19. Ibid., p. 152.

the threshold of the future, gripped in those very dogmas and claims of privileged access to truth that have been responsible for creating some of the most bitter conflicts dividing the earth's inhabitants." And it cited "the horrors being visited upon hapless populations today by outbursts of fanaticism that shame the name of religion."[20]

How are these principles of religious unity relevant to the protection of human rights? First, they indicate that there are no religious grounds for denying anyone freedom of religion or justifying discrimination against any religion or its members. Second, they suggest that all the world's religions have a critical role to play in working together to promote the realization of human rights, which is in fact the realization of those highest moral ideals at the core of every religion's teachings.

Social Reforms Necessary to Safeguard Universal Respect for Human Rights

What are some of the specific social reforms necessary to safeguard universal respect for human rights that all the world's religions can together advocate according to the Bahá'í perspective? First of all, the Bahá'í teachings are supportive of efforts like the adoption of the Universal Declaration of Human Rights by the United Nations and the discussion of the Universal Declaration of Human Rights by the World's Religions at this conference because they insist on the need to articulate global standards of human rights. Indeed, as 'Abdu'l-Bahá points out, "Bahá'u'lláh taught that an equal standard of human rights must be recognized and adopted. In the estimation of God all men are equal; there is no distinction or preferment for any soul in the dominion of

20. The Universal House of Justice, Letter Addressed to the World's Religious Leaders, April 2002, p. 3, available at http://info.bahai.orgpdf/letter_april2002_english.pdf.

His justice and equity."[21] Such standards can serve not only as a common benchmark by which to identify and remedy human rights violations, but also as an inspiration to take continuous and resolute action to promote the human rights of all members of the global human family.

Second, from a Bahá'í perspective, because we are all interdependent members of a global community, the responsibility to protect human rights lies with each individual as well as with governments. Thus, on the one hand, 'Abdu'l-Bahá insists that each of us as individuals must "have regard for the rights of others."[22] On the other hand, he proclaims that governments must ensure "the free exercise of the individual's rights, and the security of his person and property."[23] The Bahá'í teachings clearly underline the need for appropriate national and international laws that not only guarantee fundamental human rights, but also provide legal recourse for human rights victims. In this regard, 'Abdu'l-Bahá affirms that under appropriate laws protecting rights and ensuring the equal enjoyment of rights, aggrieved individuals "may justly demand human rights but without resort to force and violence."[24] And he insists on the imperative of providing human rights victims with legal rights of appeal.[25]

Third, the Bahá'í writings indicate, in keeping with Bahá'u'lláh's teaching of the oneness of humankind, that humanity must develop a global system of enforcement of international legal norms, including those concerning human rights, to supplement national enforcement systems. Indeed,

---

21. 'Abdu'l-Bahá, *The Promulgation of Universal Peace*, p. 182.
22. 'Abdu'l-Bahá, *The Secret of Divine Civilization*, 2nd edn., tr. Marzieh Gail (Wilmette, Ill.: Bahá'í Publishing Trust, 1970), p. 40.
23. Ibid., p. 115.
24. 'Abdu'l-Bahá, *The Promulgation of Universal Peace*, p. 238.
25. See 'Abdu'l-Bahá, *The Secret of Divine Civilization*, p. 18.

Bahá'u'lláh called upon the leaders of the world to establish a worldwide system of collective security as an essential means for preserving peace, in which every nation would agree, in a binding treaty, to come to the military aid of any other nation that was unjustly attacked. He also implied that such a system might be employed to dissuade and if necessary immobilize those governments that inflict tyranny upon their people. He wrote that the leaders of the world should unite "to shield mankind from the onslaught of tyranny."[26]

Fourth, and finally, however, the Bahá'í teachings recognize that no political or legal system alone, however well-intentioned or meritorious in design, can succeed in eradicating the scourge of human rights atrocities that today blemishes global society without a radical transformation in human hearts. This individual spiritual transformation, in turn, can only be brought about through education that is at once spiritually-inspired and universal. Bahá'u'lláh affirms, "Regard man as a mine rich in gems of inestimable value. Education can, alone, cause it to reveal its treasures, and enable mankind to benefit therefrom."[27] He states, further, "of all the arts and sciences, set the children to studying those which will result in advantage to man, will ensure his progress and elevate his rank. Thus the noisome odours of lawlessness will be dispelled, and thus through the high endeavours of the nation's leaders, all will live cradled, secure and in peace."[28] Universal moral education must aim at helping all children and adults not only acquire an academic knowledge of human rights, but also, and more importantly, learn to see in the face of every other human being the radiant light of

26. Bahá'u'lláh, *Tablets of Bahá'u'lláh*, p. 165.

27. Bahá'u'lláh, *Gleanings*, p. 260.

28. Bahá'u'lláh, *Tablets of Bahá'u'lláh*, pp. 168-69.

God. In this way they can be inspired to consecrate their energies to bettering the lives of others and upholding and defending their human rights.

Some Comments and Suggestions Relating to the Draft Universal Declaration of Human Rights by the World's Religions

The points I have just made that, in my personal view, form essential elements of a Bahá'í conception of human rights have certain implications for the text of the draft Universal Declaration of Human Rights by the World's Religions under consideration at this conference. First, as I have already noted, the Bahá'í teachings support this important kind of endeavour, one aimed both at articulating a universal standard of human rights and at highlighting the shared moral teachings of the world's religions relating to human rights and fostering their collaboration in promoting human rights.

In addition, these perspectives, in my personal opinion, have implications for particular articles of the draft Declaration. For example, in the light of the critical role of religiously-inspired moral principles in fostering greater respect for human rights, consideration might be given to rephrasing the third preambular paragraph in a more positive way, so that it might read:

> Whereas the world religions are positive resources for human rights and ought to be turned to as sources of guidance and inspiration in the conceptualization and implementation of human rights. . . .

Second, perhaps another preambular paragraph could be added affirming the principle of the unity of the human family as a moral foundation for upholding the human rights of all. Third, concerning Article 26, consideration could be given to adding a paragraph encouraging education aimed at cultivating understanding between members of different religions, with an emphasis on education in the moral principles shared by all world religions. Finally, another suggestion is to add a new paragraph to Article 29, relating to duties, which would clearly affirm that everyone has a duty to promote and help protect the human rights of others.

Conclusion

In closing, I have suggested in this paper that from a Bahá'í perspective the realization of human rights around the globe after the events of 11 September will require a new level of co-operation among members of different religions to identify those core beliefs in humanity's spiritual dignity that they have in common and to act on these beliefs to uphold human rights for all. The effective implementation of human rights standards requires the insights provided by this shared perspective of the world's religions. The prospects for widespread acceptance of such a unified perspective may today appear dim because of the prevalence of divisive religious dogmas and terrorist acts and other human rights violations committed under the banner of religion. However, the Bahá'í teachings are emphatic that in this epoch of human civilization the universal enjoyment of human rights will, thanks to the efforts of enlightened governmental and religious leaders, eventually become a reality.

5

Christian Missionary Activities in Turkey: Myth or Reality?

Mustafa Köylü

THE relationship between Muslims and Christians goes back to the advent of Islam, namely to the sixth century, and it has continued till date. When we look at these relationships between them we see that while in the beginning, they were very peaceful, later, because of some political and economic reasons, they turned very hostile. As a result of this quarrel, the crusaders continued to be active for about two hundred years (1096–1270). In fact, there are some important similarities between Christianity and Islam as compared with other world religions. First of all, they have a belief in God and the hereafter; they have a belief in the concept of salvation; they have sacred books. In addition to these similarities, both of them accept themselves as a divine religion and a true guidance for human beings. Therefore, although there are some differences in terms of the spreading of their faiths, both the followers of these religions aim to convert people of other faiths to their own religions. The belief in the supremacy of their respective religions and the endeavour of converting people to Islam or Christianity has continued in different ways even to this day.

In this paper, I will mainly talk about the missionary activities in Turkey. In order to do this, I will present first very briefly the religious history of the Turkish people. Secondly, I will touch on the history of Christian missionary activities in the Ottoman State. Thirdly, I will examine the Christian missionary activities and the methods used by them in modern Turkey. Lastly, I will evaluate the results of these missionary activities in terms of the Turkish Constitution.

A Short Religious History of Turkish Nation

Before becoming Muslims, Turks followed various religious beliefs and practices. In their original Central Asian homelands, they followed Shamanistic practices. They also came into contact with Buddhism, Manichaeism and Nestorian Christianity in the course of time. However, when they started moving westward and encountered Muslim Arabs, they met Islam, which made a greater impact upon them and thereby changed the course of history.

The War of Manzikert (Malazgirt), which took place between the Seljuks under Alparslan and the Byzantines in 1071, near Lake Van in Eastern Anatolia, became a turning point in Turkish history. This victory opened to the Turkish people the doors of Anatolia and made the land of Anatolia Muslim. Seljuk dominance in Anatolia lasted for two centuries and established a brilliant Anatolian civilization which still influences events today.

After the Seljuks were defeated by the Mongols, the Ottomans gained dominance in Anatolia and established a new state in 1299 in Western Anatolia, bordering on the Byzantine territory. Although Turkish people have established many states through their history, the most influential and the one lasting the longest was the Ottoman State. It was established in 1299 and collapsed in 1923. When we examine the Ottoman State from the religious point of view, it is seen that while the Ottoman State was basically an Islamic state and manifestations of their Islamic faith were evident in all aspects of their lives, it recognized religious differences, and did not distinguish between members of any religion on racial or religious grounds. So, Turks, Arabs, Kurds, and other nationalities were treated as citizens of the Ottoman State. The golden age of the Ottoman's lasted from 1451 to 1566 and they achieved their greatest glories during this period.[1]

As a result of both internal and external reasons, the Ottoman State began to decline from the beginning of the seventeenth century.[2] The Ottomans had to face up to the West, particularly with France, as a result of military and scientific failures. As a result of this confrontation, French ideas on political, legal philosophy and the place of religion in the state began to penetrate into Turkey. Those ideas, and the growing European interference in Ottoman affairs, led Turkish intellectuals to debate the Ottoman response to the challenge of the West. At this point, while some Turkish intellectuals grasped the concept of *nationalism* and argued that religion could be regarded as a matter for the private belief of the individual, the others held the view that *Islam* should be involved in every aspect of life and form the foundation of the state and society. However, the idea of nationalism and the attempt to reduce religion to only the private belief of individual, met with fierce resistance. Overall, three rival remedies were offered for the empire's ills, each offering a different basis on which unity might be achieved. In 1904, these were listed as: *Ottomanism* — a common citizenship and loyalty of all subjects of the empire without regard to religion or race, as had been the case in the past; *Islamism* (pan-

---

1. See for information about the social and technological advances during the Ottoman time, Ziya Kazici, *Islam Müesseseleri Tarihi* (İstanbul: Kayhan Yay., 1991), pp. 217-70; Hüseyin Atay, *Osmanlilarda Yüksek Din Eğitimi* (İstanbul: Dergah Yay., 1983), pp. 75-130.
2. Amiran Kurtkan Bilgiseven, *Eğitim Sosyolojisi* (İstanbul: Türk Dünyasi Araştirmalari Vakfi Yayinlari, 1987), pp.188-98.

Islamism) — the union of all Muslim people in the world; and *Turkism* (or pan-Turkism) — the unity of people speaking the Turkish language. At the end, neither Ottomanism nor Islamism could prevail against the rising tide of nationalism, which caused the collapse of the Ottoman State, and led the Turkish people to establish a new state, "a secular, democratic, and social legislative" called the Republic of Turkey.[3] Of course, this main change in the structure of the state affected religious life and the religious thinking of Turkish people too.

Although many reforms were actualized in the new state,[4] the most important reform which affected all aspects of society was the acceptance of secularism. As Richard F. Nyrop wrote: "As Islam had formed the identity of Ottoman subject and empire, so secularism would form the identity of the new Turkish man and nation."[5] With the acceptance of secularism, religion was separated from the legal, educational and cultural life of Turkish people. The state not only declared itself as a secular one, but also took severe precautions to control and direct religious affairs and to keep them out of the political sphere. As Elisabeth Ozdalga states, Turkish secularism was not only concerned about keeping the state apparatus free of religious influences, it also sets out to restrict the influence of

3. J. D. Norton, "The Turks and Islam," in *The World's Religions*, ed. Steward Sutherland et al. (Boston: G. K.: Hall and Co., 1988), pp. 390-98; see for more information about the views of Turkism and Islamism, Ziya Gökalp, *Türkleşmek, Islamlaşmak, Muasirlaşmak* (İstanbul: Türk Klasikleri, 2004); Recai Doğan, *İslamcilarin Eğitim Görüşleri* (Ankara, 1999), pp. 11-32.

4. See for reforms made in Turkey, Howard A. Reed, "Revival of Islam in Secular Turkey," *The Middle East Journal*, vol. 8, pt 3 (1954), p. 269.

5. Richard F. Nyrop, *Area Handbook for the Republic of Turkey* (2nd edn.) (Washington D. C.: U.S. Government Printing Office, 1973), p. 120.

religion as a belief and faith system.[6] Through the reform of secularism and similar measures, in the words of Norton, "Islam had been made a department of the state; the men of religion had become minor religious servants."[7] The aim of the ministry of Religious Affairs, which was set up under direct control of the prime minister in 1924, also coincided with this.[8] Today, the principle of secularism has been applied in a very different way in Turkey in comparison with other secular states in the world.

The History of Missionary Activities in Turkey

As I said before, the Ottoman State included many different peoples, religions and cultures. Among them the Christians and Jews had a special place, for these people were accepted as "the People of the Book" by Muslims.[9] Treating the People of the Book well is a Qur'anic imperative. In addition, since

---

6. Elisabeth Ozdalga, "On Islamic Revivalism and Radicalism in Turkey," in *The Influence on the Frankfurt School on Contemporary Theology*, ed. James Reimer (Lewiston: The Edwin Mellen Press, 1992), p. 332.
7. See Şerif Mardin, "Turkey: Islam and Westernization," in *Religions and Societies: Asia and Middle East*, ed. Carlo Caldarola (Berlin and New York: Mouton Pub., 1982), p. 181.
8. Its purpose was defined as follows: "To direct the affairs pertaining to the beliefs of the Muslim religion and to the foundation of worship and morals; to enlighten the population on the subject of religion and to administer places of worship." In fact, its task, as Norton and Mardin have said, was to ensure that religion was to be used in the service of the state and to control all training for religious offices as well as the salaries and appointments of all religious officials. Norton, "The Turks and Islam," p. 403; see also Mardin, "Turkey: Islam and Westernization," p. 179.
9. In fact, this is a mandatory Qur'anic teaching. See for some Qur'anic verses about the people of the book: 2: 105, 109; 3: 69-72, 75, 98, 99, 110, 113, 199; 4: 123, 153, 159, 171; 5: 15, 19, 47, 59, 65, 68, 77; 28: 12; 29: 46; 33: 26; 57: 29; 59: 2, 11; 98: 1, 6. Therefore, all Muslims believe the prophecy of Jesus Christ and accept the Bible as a divine book.

Turkish people lived in a multi-national, multi-cultural and multi-religious society, this pluralistic environment led them to be more tolerant and encouraged a pluralist attitude and behaviour towards the other religions and their adherents. Furthermore, Turkish religiosity usually represented a mystical or "Sufistic" character, which has more tolerant and pluralistic dimensions. For example, Mawlana Jalal al-Din al-Rumi, Muhyi al-Din Ibn Arabi, and Yunus Emre lived in Anatolia and had a permanent effect on the religious thinking and understanding of Anatolian people. Their views are so original and well known that even some contemporary Western philosophers such as John Hick quote their ideas several times, such as "the lamps are different, but the light is the same."[10] As a result of this understanding, all religious buildings and cultures were strictly protected by the Ottoman State. Even today it is possible to see churches, synagogues and other religious buildings in many cities of Turkey.

While the Ottoman State was powerful, there was no problem concerning the minority groups in the state. They paid their taxes; they did their duties towards the state, and lived very peacefully with Muslim people. There was a great religious freedom for them. However, when the Ottoman State began to decline, the attitudes of the minority groups began to change. Minority groups in Ottoman State or foreign states began to open new schools in the land of Ottoman State. To some, the opening of these schools became a turning point in the history of Ottoman State. The main cause responsible for the decline and collapse of the Ottoman State were these schools, for these foreign schools did not work as educational

---

10. Cafer Sadik Yaran, "Non-Exclusivist Attitudes Towards Other Religions in Recent Turkish Theology and Philosophy of Religion," in *Change and Essence*, ed. Sinasi Gündüz and C. S. Yaran (Washington, D.C.: Council for Research in Values and Philosophy, 2005), pp. 7-8.

settings, but worked for the benefit and interests of foreign countries. These schools were always supported by powerful states for their own interests. As a result of the foreign political and missionary activities, the minority groups began to think that they were different nations and had different religions and cultures. Foreign countries set out to acquire such minority status for their own religions and countries. Foreign countries always supported minorities to build their own enclaves in the land of Ottoman State. The aim to achieve an independent state became the main aim of every minority group in the Ottoman State. For example, curriculum of the Byzantium Greek school in Island Cunda near to Edremit dated at 1884, included the following items:

1. To present Turkish people to Greek people as an eternal enemy.
2. To make Turkish people weak economically.
3. To damage Turkish dignity in every subject in the eyes of European Countries.
4. To make Turkish people weak religiously, morally, nationally, and traditionally.
5. To destroy Turkish youth.
6. To re-take (conquer) Istanbul.
7. To corrupt the relationship between the Turkish people and the state.
8. To cause Turkish people fall a great difficult position in every field of occupation.
9. To gain some Turkish people for using their own interest through bribery and corruption.[11]

---

11. Necdet Sevinç *Ajan Okullari,* İstanbul 1975, pp, 192-96; Haydaroğlu, İlknur P. Haydaroğlu, *Osmanli–Imparatorluğu'nda Yabanci Okullar* (Ankara: Ocak Yayinlari, 1993), p. 168.

The foreign schools were so widespread that almost all foreign countries such as France, England, USA, Italy, Germany, Australia, Russia, Iran, and Bulgaria opened new schools in the land of Ottoman State. The first foreign school was opened in 1454 in Istanbul by Greeks as "Fener Rum." Later, Saint Benoit was opened in 1583 and Sankt George in 1629, in Istanbul. The number of foreign schools increased slowly in the land of Ottoman State in the beginning. However, the number of these schools began to increase in the years of 1840s. In 1900-25, the numbers of these schools reached very high levels. During this period, Greeks had 59; Armenians 37, Jews 21, Protestants 13, France 72, England 83 (only in Istanbul), America 465 (in 1845 had only 7 schools), Italy 24, Germany 7, Russia 44, Iran 3, and Bulgaria 212.[12]

As to the number of foreign students, according to the state records in 1900s, there were 17,846 Byzantine Greek, 1253 Armenian, 1781 Italian, 1048 French, 370 Bulgarian and 104 Jewish students.[13] In fact, not only the children of Christian or Jewish people did go to these schools but also the elite group of Ottomans went to these schools. Thus Muslim students were also affected by foreign thoughts. While some of these schools were theological seminaries, others were secular schools, and the quality of education offered by them was very high compared with *madrasas*. These schools gave importance to three things: (1) the quality of education, (2) political activities, and (3) missionary activities.

In the beginning, the aims of religious groups coming to the land of Ottoman State since the thirteenth century (1220)

---

12. For general information about the effects of foreign schools, see Tuncer Günay, *Misyoner Örgütleri ve Misyoner Faaliyetleri* (Ankara: Ankara Ticaret Odasi, 2004), pp. 185-300; Haydaroğlu, Osmanli İmparatorluğu'nda Yabanci Okullar, pp. 89-98.
13. Haydaroğlu, Osmanli İmparatorluğu'nda Yabanci Okullar, p. 96.

were to give religious education for the minority groups, to acquire new followers to their own religious sects, and to educate young people in missionary activities. However, over time they forgot their religious aims, and began to work for political aims. The aims of missionaries can be summarized in general as follows:

1. To proclaim the teaching of Jesus Christ for those who are not Christians, to teach the Bible to those who do not know about it.
2. To provide religious services for those who belonged to the Church of Eastern Catholic.
3. To unite the Church of East and Rome, and for this purpose, to make East Christians Catholic.
4. To detach the minority groups from being citizens of Ottoman State, and help to establish their own states in the land of Ottoman State.
5. To teach Christianity to all Christians who live under the rule of Ottoman State.
6. To educate priest and nun for the religious services.[14]
7. To adversely influence the Turkish and Muslim students in terms of religion and to alienate them from their own nations.

How could they achieve these aims? In order to achieve their aims, they chose the following ways:

1. To establish churches and monasteries in the cities.
2. To prepare conferences.
3. To establish charity institutions: These institutions also opened many schools. For example, an English charity institution, C.M.S. had 75 schools with 4600 students in 1903.

---

14. Haydaroğlu, Osmanli İmparatorluğu'nda Yabanci Okullar, p. 185.

4. To establish some associations that contribute to make their members Christian. One of the most important associations was the organization of tracking. These organizations were established by missionaries at foreign schools. Orthodox and Muslim students were taken to these tracking organizations. Furthermore, in order to graduate from these schools, every student had to participate in these organizations. In these organizations, they easily propagated their thoughts and tried to convert Muslim students to Christianity.
5. To open dormitories for orphans.
6. To help poor children and people.
7. To provide for job for needy people.
8. To diagnose the sick and help for buying their medicine.
9. To open accommodation.
10. To teach French.
11. To open theological seminaries for educating nuns and priests.[15]

The main purpose of all these works was to gain the trust of the Turkish people. They are prevented from all kinds of activities that might be misunderstood. They approached Muslim people very positively, even in religious matters. For example, they never used the words of "the Son of God" among Muslim population. Regarding this matter, Charles R. Watson wrote: "Missionaries should be innocent like pigeons. But it is not to say that they should not be cunning like snakes."[16] The most appropriate places for missionary activities

---

15. Haydaroğlu, Osmanli İmparatorluğu'nda Yabanci Okullar, p. 185-86.
16. Mustafa Halidi, Ömer Ferruh, *İslam Ülkelerinde Misyonerlik ve Emperyalizm*, çev. Osman Şekerci, 1968, p. 59.

were schools. Because of that they gave great importance for opening schools. On this point, Jesuits said: "The first missionary is school."[17]

While all foreign countries sent some missionaries to the lands of Ottoman State and opened new schools, America had a special place in these kinds of activities. Although the Americans came to the land of the Ottoman State after the Europeans (1840s), they opened many schools in a very short time. In 1870, they opened 33 schools in various cities and enrolled 880 students in just 30 years. Between the years of 1870-1900, they opened 233 schools and the student numbers stood at 17,776. American missionaries made the following evaluation concerning these activities: While the years of 1820-39 were accepted as a "period of preparation," the years of 1840-70 were described as "the period of settling," the years of 1870-1900 were glorified as "the period of harvest."[18] In addition to these schools, the Americans established a hospital called The Mason Memorial Hospital. This hospital was under the rule of masons and missionaries. As of 1893, there were 1,317 American missionaries, out of which 223 came from America, the remaining 1,094 were educated Armenians in the Ottoman State.[19]

Missionaries had 436 prayer places in Turkey. These places employed 1,006 people of whom 228 were priests. In addition to the schools, churches and chapels, missionaries also opened some publishing houses. Until 1883, three million Bibles and

17. Halidi, Ferruh, *İslam Ülkelerinde Misyonerlik ve Emperyalizm*, p. 85.
18. See for more information, İskender Oymak et al., "Elaziğ, Tunceli ve Bingöl Çevresinde Misyonerlik Faaliyetleri," *Dinler Tarihçileri Gözüyle Türkiye'de Misyonerlik*, TÜDTAD, Ankara, 2005, (121-31), p. 122, endnote, number 11.
19. Haydaroğlu, Osmanli İmparatorluğu'nda Yabanci Okullar, p. 188; Şamil Mutlu, *Osmanli Devleti'nde Misyoner Okullari* (İstanbul: Gökkubbe Yayinlari, 2005), p. 145 vd.

four million religious books were distributed to the people. Until 1881, a total 725 various religious books were published in the land of Ottoman State. Only 10 per cent of these books were school books. Americans spent 285,000 dollars every year and most of the money was spent for Armenians.[20] At the end, the nineteenth century became the "golden age" for Christian missionary activities.[21]

The political activities of missionaries were more important and dangerous than their pure religious activities. In the beginning, the missionaries wanted to serve only in the religious areas. However, later they changed their attitudes and began to work in the political sphere. In this process, they used, even abused, the minority groups in the land of Ottoman State. They used schools and other associations as a means to gain their true aims. Their true aims were to detach the minority groups from the Ottomans, and make them establish their own states in the land of Ottoman State. They achieved their aims in four ways: (1) through missionary activities and religious propaganda, (2) through offering monetary help, (3) through opening new schools, and (4) through opening embassies.[22]

Foreign powers used all kinds of means for achieving their own aims. However, the schools and embassies had a special place, for they taught the minority groups their languages, cultures and national histories through the curriculums and

---

20. Haydaroğlu, Osmanli İmparatorluğu'nda Yabanci Okullar, pp. 188-89.

21. Ahmet Gökbel, "Sivas ve Tokat Çevresinde Misyonerlik Faalityetleri," *Dinler Tarihçileri Gözüyle Türkiye'de Misyonerlik*, TÜDTAD, Ankara, 2005, pp. 219-29.

22. For general information about missionary activities towards minority groups in Turkey, see Mustafa Erdem, "Türkiye'de Azinliklara Yönelik Misyoner Faaliyetleri," *Türkiye'de Misyonerlik Faaliyetleri* (İstanbul: Ensar Neşriyat, 2005), pp. 280-88.

helped both the students and their families in various ways. Thus, they gained sympathizers and provoked these people against the Ottoman State. In addition, these schools were opened in very strategic places such as in the heavily populated areas of minority groups, and places rich in terms of natural sources. Thus, they easily discovered the important places in the land of Ottoman State and used these sources for their own interests later. As to embassies, all foreign embassies worked for their own countries' interest. These embassies sent reports continuously about every kind of activities, events, and information in relation to the population over to their own countries. In the end, the Ottoman State collapsed. As Haydaroglu wrote:

> If Turkey in particular and Middle East in general today has an Armani, Kurt, Palestine, or an Arab problem, the main reason for these problems are the missionaries and their various activities.[23]

Current Christian Missionary Activities and Their Methods in Modern Turkey

As a result of both internal and external reasons, the Ottoman State collapsed in the first quarter of twentieth century. A new state called the Republic of Turkey was established in Anatolia. Some foreigners thought that the missionary activities might still continue and even gain more power with the establishment of a new secular state, for the state would not support or side with any religion or religious group in the country. Even a foreigner proclaimed Turkey as "the country of Bible."[24] However, the missionary activities lost important prestige and power with the establishment of the new state. An event became a turning point. When three Turkish girls

---

23. Haydaroğlu, Osmanli İmparatorluğu'nda Yabanci Okullar, p. 195.
24. H. Lukas Hieser, *Iskalanmiş Bariş* (Ankara: İletişim Yayinlari, 2005), p. 69.

became Christians in an American College in Bursa, in 1928, this school was closed and all other foreign schools were also taken under strict control.[25] During this period (1923-50) there was an important decline in missionary activities in modern Turkey. However, after the establishment of the multi-party system in Turkey (1950s), the missionary activities began to increase. They now reached a new peak recently as Turkey prepares to enter to the Union of Europe.

Now we can ask the following question: Are there really missionary activities being carried out in Turkey, as has happened before? If yes, what kinds of methods are used to evangelize the Muslim population? While some people think that there are a great number of missionaries in Turkey and if it continues this way, this may be a great threat for Turkey in the future, some people believe that that there is nothing to fear about these missionary activities. They believe that since the great majority of Turkish people are Muslims, it is not possible to convert them to Christianity. Whatever people think or say, it is a fact that there has been a growing interest concerning missionary activities in Turkey. Because of that much research has been done and many symposiums have been organized recently about this matter. In addition to these academic works, many television programmes have been organized about missionary activities. One recent symposium concerning missionary activities in Turkey was entitled the "Mission in Turkey from Perspectives of the Historians of Religions." The symposium papers were published in 2005. In this book, almost every city or area was investigated from the point of missionary activities. The remainder of this paper is mostly based on these papers.

According to all researchers in this book, there are a great number of missionaries in Turkey and this poses a real threat

25. Haydaroğlu, Osmanli İmparatorluğu'nda Yabanci Okullar, p. 138.

for the future of Turkey. For example, the organizer of this symposium, Abdurrahman Küçük writes that although the methods of missionaries may have changed, it is not possible to imagine that these activities have ended. The only things that have changed are the methods, ways, and places. As long as there are different religions and their followers, the struggle for supremacy and gaining new people will continue.[26] At this point, one can ask whether Christians have any right to convey the Christian message to a Muslim population. One could ask: Don't Muslims do the same thing in European countries or America or Canada, etc.? Aren't both religions missionary? In fact, both religions have the same mission and both of them try to gain followers from other faiths and religions. However, there are significant differences between them in terms of missional understanding and methods. According to Küçük's evaluation, Christian mission is characterized by compulsion, deception, trickery, cheating, and abuse of feelings while the Islamic mission is characterized by persuasion, clarity, sincerity, and honesty.[27] In fact, to him, this is a Qur'anic imperative.

According to some scholars, there are two kinds of missionary activities directed towards Turkish people and Turkey: religious and political missionary activities. While the first one is being carried out by some Christian groups, the other has been executed directly by some foreign states. Since

---

26. Abdurrahman Küçük, "Takdim," *Dinler Tarihçileri Gözüyle Türkiye'de Misyonerlik*, TÜDTAD, Ankara, 2005, pp. 9-15.
27. Abdurrahman Küçük, "Misyonerlik Nedir? Misyonerlik ile Tebliğ Arasindaki Fark," *Dinler Tarihçileri Gözüyle Türkiye'de Misyonerlik*, TÜDTAD, Ankara, 2005, (19-33), p. 25. See also David A. Kerr, "Islamic *Da'wa* and Christian Mission: Towards a Comparative Analysis," *International Review of Mission* (Apr 2000) 89, no. 353, pp. 150-71.

the initiation of the process of entering into the Union of Europe, especially in the context of the "Adaptation Packets," in 2003, Turkey has given many privileges to the European countries. According to the new regulations, foreign countries might buy real estate and properties for religious, cultural, social, and medical constructions. Thus, they might easily build new churches, and other religious foundations in cities. In addition, the name of mosque has been changed to a "place of worship" according to the Law, (the Law of Construction no. 3194). After the passing of this law, local administrators will have to give permission for all kinds of constructions.[28] Thus, to some, missionary activities are not an innocent movement. It involves "spiritual terror," which has political, cultural, and intelligence dimensions. This movement goes back in history to the thirteenth century and has continued to date in a very organized and planned way. Today, there are missionary activities at the back of "the Great Middle East Project." Therefore, this movement has to be forbidden immediately. For no country gives permission to anybody for dividing the country or destroying the unity of its people. As a result, missionary activities are not a movement of conveying or teaching the message of Jesus Christ, but a movement that perpetrates many tricks and abuses in the name of religion.[29]

After this short discussion about missionary activities, we can pass on to the methods used by missionaries in Turkey. There are of course many methods and ways for promoting Christian propaganda. However, the following are the most used and influential methods.

---

28. Küçük, "Misyonerlik Nedir?" p. 29.
29. Küçük, "Misyonerlik Nedir?" pp. 30, 33; Mehmet Aydin, "Hiristiyan Misyonerliğinin Başlangici, Gelişimi ve Hedefleri," (pp. 35-47), *Dinler Tarihçileri Gözüyle Türkiye'de Misyonerlik*, TÜDTAD, Ankara, 2005, p. 47.

The first method used by missionaries for spreading the faith of Christianity is Internet. Recep Kiliç who investigated these kinds of Internet websites directed towards Turkish people and Islam, found 60 such websites.[30] To him, there are two kinds of Internet methods used concerning Christianity. The first one aims to give information about the faith of Christianity and to teach the followers of Christianity. This is quite normal and every religion may and does pursue these kinds of activities. These websites give information about the faith principles of Christianity, the question of salvation, the content of the Bible, the questions asked most and their answers, some contemporary questions such as the relationship between Christianity and other religions, interreligious dialogue, sexuality, homosexuality, war and peace in Christianity, the history of Turkish Christianity, the legal rights of the followers of Jesus in Turkey, some problems met by Protestant Christians in Turkey and their legal rights in international arena.

The other group of website is related to Islam and the Turkish people. These websites (six) accuse Islam and Muslims very severely. They show Islam as an enemy for Christianity. Although they touch many topics, the following are very important in terms of missionary activities. These websites assert that Anatolian land belongs to the Christian population and therefore it is sacred. There are some heavy accusations concerning the Qur'an and the Prophet Muhammad. For example, there are some topics in this website such as "Some contradictions in the Qur'an," "Some verses against science from the Qur'an," Some *hadiths* that are contradictory to the

30. While Recep Kiliç founded 60 websites concerning missionary activities towards Turkey, according to another research done by Şerif Bayrak, there are 178 Internet websites for missionary activities. See Oymak et al., "Elaziğ, Tunceli ve Bingöl Çevresinde Misyonerlik Faaliyetleri," p. 124.

science," and many other accusations concerning the teaching of the Qur'an are propagated. In another website, the rights of Christians and missionaries from point of both national and international arena are described.[31] Overall, the aim of these websites is to produce some doubts in the minds of sincere Muslims concerning the basic sources of Islam and its teaching, and then to suggest Christianity as the real solution. In addition, it is argued that the geography of Turkey belongs to the Christian nations.

The second method used by Christian missionaries for converting Muslim people to Christianity is to distribute the Bible and other Christian documents along with 100 dollars. This is one of the most common methods used by Christian missionaries. There are several steps involved in delivering the Bible. First of all, they want to identify the people to whom it should be sent. For this purpose, they take home addresses using Internet or newspaper advertisements. Once the addresses are secured, a questionnaire is administered to the householders. If they find that those people are willing to receive the Bible, they send the Bible along with other religious documents. They sometimes even deliver a normal letter to the houses that includes the following note: "If you want a Bible, we can immediately send it to you free. We will also find you a job or meet your needs. Please make contact with us." If you write them to send a Bible, they send a Bible and place hundred dollars inside the Bible. They sometimes hand over 100-200 dollars directly, or provide some food or clothes for those who are in need.[32] As of 2003, some newspaper claims

---

31. Recep Kiliç, "Türkçe Internet Ortaminda Misyonerlik Araştirmasi," *Dinler Tarihçileri Gözüyle Türkiye'de Misyonerlik*, (103-10) TÜDTAD, Ankara, 2005, pp. 103-08.

32. Hüseyin Yilmaz, "Van ve Ağri Çevresinde Misyonerlik," *Dinler Tarihçileri Gözüyle Türkiye'de Misyonerlik*, (133-50) TÜDTAD, Ankara, 2005, s. 136; Kenan Has, "Çorum-Yozgat Çevresinde Misyonerlik Faaliyetleri," *Dinler Tarihçileri Gözüyle Türkiye'de Misyonerlik*, TÜDTAD, Ankara, 2005, (231-41.), p. 237.

that five million books (including the Bible) have been distributed in Turkey. In addition, Protestant missionaries assert that by 2020 at least 10 per cent of Muslim population will be Christian and one million copies of the Bible would have been delivered in Turkey.[33]

The missionaries not only send the Bible to these people, but also offer some Bible courses to them. While they give Bible courses, they notice some important points. In the beginning, they use very respectful and polite language towards Islam and Muslims. Later, they compare Islamic faith and practices with those of Christianity and argue that Christianity gives great importance on love, peace and compassion. Lastly, they discuss some Islamic topics such as the sources of Islam (the Qur'an and the *hadith*) war, the question of equality between man and woman, the situation of Muslim countries, etc.

All of these books are in Turkish and published in Turkey by various publishing houses.[34] The first course is called as "Alfa courses." This course is for beginners. Later, the courses are offered according to the level of people.

The third method is to give scholarship to high school and undergraduate students attending the various universities

33. Ahmet Arpad, *Cumhuriyet Gazetesi*, 17.08.2003; *Zaman Gazetesi*, 31.12.2004; *Takvim Gazetesi*, 27.02.2005. See also Uslu et al., "Malatya ve Adiyaman Çevresinde Misyonerlik Faaliyetleri," p. 182.

34. Some of these publishing houses are Kitab-i Mukaddes Şirketi, Kucak Yayincilik, Lütuf Yayincilik, Yaşam Yayincilik, Yeni Yaşam Yayincilik, Sevgi Yayinlari, Kaya Yayinicilik, Kayra Yayincilik, Güçlü Yayincilik, Zirve Yayincilik, Müjde Yayincilik, Logos Yayincilik, see Oymak et al., "Elaziğ, Tunceli ve Bingöl Çevresinde Misyonerlik Faaliyetleri," p. 124; M. Numan Malkoç, "Türkiye'de Protestan Misyonerliği," *Türkiye'de Misyonerlik Faaliyetleri,* (161-93) İstanbul: Ensar Neşriyat, pp, 185-86; M. Numan Malkoç, "İstanbul ve Çevresinde Misyonerlik," *Dinler Tarihçileri Gözüyle Türkiye'de Misyonerlik*, TÜDTAD, Ankara, 2005, (245-68), pp. 256-57.

of about 100-200 dollars each month. For this purpose, some students are chosen and given 200 dollars. These students become pastors or priests and then try to find new students to include in their group. These students mostly choose their friends from Kurdish or Alawi children. When they choose these young, they use the psychology of minority or religious differences. However, while they do this, they make a very careful investigation concerning the region. For this purpose, they prefer the eastern part of Turkey where mostly Kurdish and Alawi people live, or the big cities such as Istanbul, İzmir, Adana, Samsun and Trabzon. In order to start these activities, first a few missionary people come to that region, investigate that region in terms of minority groups, strategic point of view, appropriate persons, etc. and after deciding that this region is appropriate for Christian missionary activities, they begin to work for their aims.[35]

They choose Alawi youth because they claim that Alawiyyun is a different type of living and it is completely different from teaching of Islam. There are many similarities between Christianity and Alawi faith. They claim that there are some similarities in terms of Trinity/Allah, Muhammad and Ali, twelve apostles/*imams*; baptism/ablution, priests/ Bektashi fathers; Paul/Hossein (grandchild of the Prophet in terms of how their life ended).[36] Thus, they think that it is easier to win over Alawi youth to their faiths.[37] For instance, they say just as you may see and accept Jesus Christ, we see

35. Ali Refat Özkan and Kemal Polat, "Erzurum, Erzincan, Kars ve Iğdir Yöresinde Misyonerlik," *Dinler Tarihçileri Gözüyle Türkiye'de Misyonerlik*, (113-19) TÜDTAD, Ankara, 2005, p.115; Yilmaz, "Van ve Ağri Çevresinde Misyonerlik," p. 137.

36. Talip Atalay, "Diyarbakir ve Mardin'de Misyonerlik Faaliyetleri," *Dinler Tarihçileri Gözüyle Türkiye'de Misyonerlik*, (141-50) TÜDTAD, Ankara, 2005, p. 149.

37. Oymak et al., "Elaziğ, Tunceli ve Bingöl Çevresinde Misyonerlik Faaliyetleri," p. 125.

and accept Ali (the third caliphate). Therefore we are closer to you than Sunnite Muslims.[38] In addition, they say Alawi and Kurdish youth that

> You are not Turks, because of that Turkey does not give you your religious and minorities rights. If you became Christian, your reputation would be raised and you would be honoured by Christian countries. In case Turkey enters the European Union, all of your rights will be granted to you.[39]

The fourth method is to give language or computer courses for Turkish students. One of the most common methods used by Christian missionaries is to open language courses or to give courses at schools or universities. A foreign language, English in particular, is very important for underdeveloped countries. Since they know this fact, they come voluntarily or for very low salary for teaching English. In fact, they are not real teachers, but since English is their native language, they can use this method very easily. These teachers come from abroad and they are mostly missionary oriented. When the administrators realize that these teachers are indulging in missionary activities, they stop them from teaching at state schools. But it is not possible to do the same with private schools. They can hire these teachers. In addition to these language courses, some missionaries open study centres for elementary or middle schools' children. Music, picture teachers and a pastor are provided at the centres. These elementary students are brought from their families by cars in the morning, and they are picked up by their families in the evening. Of course, they not only teach the school subjects, but also

---

38. Atalay, "Diyarbakir ve Mardin'de Misyonerlik Faaliyetleri," p. 163.
39. Uslu et al., "Malatya ve Adiyaman Çevresinde Misyonerlik Faaliyetleri," p. 192.

propagate Christianity among these little children.[40]

The fifth method is to open a "house church" in the cities.[41] Since it is a little bit difficult to open new churches and to run these churches, they prefer to open new house churches. By doing this, they have two aims: First, nobody raises doubts about these houses. Secondly, it is very economical and easy to use them for their aims. House churches are opened in two ways: Either Christian missionaries themselves open these houses and invite students or other people to these places, or they hire these houses for the students and pay their salaries. This way is more subtle and safer because no one is suspicious of these activities. But in fact, these houses are used for the aim of missionary activities. For example, it is supposed that in Van there are 30 houses and in Malatya there are 43 houses that are being used for this purpose.[42]

In these houses, they not only teach the faith of Christianity but also criticise Muslims and their sacred values. However, they do not do this in the beginning of the course. First, they talk about the Qur'anic verses related to Jesus Christ and they say that the Qur'an accepts Jesus as a true prophet, and there are many similarities between Christianity and Islam. But, later they begin to discuss, compare and attack Islam.[43] They claim that Islam is a religion of war and violence. If Muslim nations

---

40. Özkan, Polat, "Erzurum, Erzincan, Kars ve Iğdir Yöresinde Misyonerlik," 115; Yilmaz, "Van ve Ağri Çevresinde Misyonerlik," p. 136.

41. Ahmet Aras, "Konya ve Çevresinde Misyonerlik," *Dinler Tarihçileri Gözüyle Türkiye'de Misyonerlik*, (211-213) TÜDTAD, Ankara, 2005, p. 212.

42. Yilmaz, "Van ve Ağri Çevresinde Misyonerlik,", p. 135; Uslu et al., "Malatya ve Adiyaman Çevresinde Misyonerlik Faaliyetleri," p. 183..

43. Uslu et al., "Malatya ve Adiyaman Çevresinde Misyonerlik Faaliyetleri," p. 192.

are backward today, the main reason for this backwardness is their religion. The Qur'an is not an original book. There are many contradictions in it. While the prophets before Jesus Christ were true, the Prophet Muhammad is a false prophet. Muhammad married many women; this is not right for a prophet. In addition to these accusations, they accuse the Presidency of Religious Affairs and its members. They say that *imams* are forgers and bribe-takers. The Presidency of Religious Affairs is a puppet and has some contact with Iran and Saudi Arabia.[44]

The sixth method is to organize the tourist groups for visiting some important places. Recently, the most common method is to organize the tourist groups for visiting some important places for Christians. These people, archaeologists or the historians of art claim that they visit natural and historical places. At first glance, it is seen that there is no problem about these kinds of visiting. However, when it is investigated these regions are not chosen by chance, they are chosen very deliberately. When these people visit these regions, they say to those who live over there that originally; their ancestors lived there, thus, they try to make friends with those people and claim that those regions belonged to themselves.[45] Or they say to the local people that "these buildings belonged to our ancestors, Turks made you Muslims by using force. We invite you to Christianity that was the religion of your ancestors."[46] If you are today backward, the

44. Uslu et al., "Malatya ve Adiyaman Çevresinde Misyonerlik Faaliyetleri," p. 183; Zeki Arslantürk, "Müzakere," *Türkiye'de Misyonerlik Faaliyetleri,* (379-403) (İstanbul: Ensar Neşriyat, 2005), p. 390.

45. Özkan, Polat, "Erzurum, Erzincan, Kars ve Iğdir Yöresinde Misyonerlik," pp. 115-116.

46. Atalay, "Diyarbakir ve Mardin'de Misyonerlik Faaliyetleri," p. 162.

reason for this is your religion, Islam. If you become Christian, you will be rich and live in prosperity.[47] In addition, they take photos of some historical churches and places, and post them on the walls, doors or sell them to the tourists. Thus, they try to emphasize Christian culture and their traditions.[48]

In addition to these tourist groups, there is also something called "faith tourism." In the name of faith tourism, some symposiums, panels and meetings are being organized. Some religious leaders from among Christians, Jews or other religions are invited to this faith tourism. They make speeches, talk, visit mosques, churches, and synagogues, and pray together, etc. They open new prayer places or "faith gardens" in strategic places.[49]

The seventh method is to help those who are poor and needy, widows, orphans, or the victims of terror. This method has been used for centuries. While this behaviour is much discredited, missionaries use all these kinds of means. First of all, the earthquakes, floods, fires, and other natural disasters are seen as a great chance for Christian missionaries. For example, in the earthquake of Marmara in 1999, Bingöl and other natural disasters, they delivered food for the needy people. The foundation of Caritas Turkey specially helped in various ways in those days. While 95 per cent of the money they paid for the needy people comes from abroad, just 5 percent of the money is collected from Catholics in Turkey. According to a report prepared by Caritas Turkey its mandate includes the following activities: (a) to develop projects after

---

47. Gökbel, "Sivas ve Tokat Çevresinde Misyonerlik Faaliyetleri," p. 229.
48. Atalay, "Diyarbakir ve Mardin'de Misyonerlik Faaliyetleri," p. 161.
49. Harun Güngör, Mustafa Ünal, Ramazan Adibelli, "Kayseri, Nevşehir ve Kirşehir Çevresinde Misyonerlik Faaliyetleri," *Dinler Tarihçileri Gözüyle Türkiye'de Misyonerlik*, (215-29) TÜDTAD, Ankara, 2005, p. 217.

earthquake, (b) to organize the affairs of immigrants and refugees, (c) to help the poor and needy people, and d) to take care of street children.[50] Thus, the target groups of Caritas Turkey are the poor, needy, socially isolated or marginalized people. But at the same time, they do not neglect to deliver the Bible and other school supplies during these disasters.[51] If these kinds of natural disasters do not take place, they help people in various ways. While some doctors diagnose the sick people without taking any money, some pharmacists also give medicine either at a cheaper rate or even free to poor people.[52] As I said above, while Caritas Turkey helped those who were in need, it did not omit to deliver the Bibles, with 100 dollars placed inside them. According to a news item during the earthquake of Sakarya (17 August 1999), thousands of Bibles were distributed and 2,500 people were Christianized through giving money in that area. And 100 embossed Turkish Bibles were sent for blind people.[53]

Thus, they try to get people's love and sympathies towards themselves. However, these offers of help are not made without ulterior motives. The following example confirms this. According to a newspaper item dated 10 April 2003, Wilbur Miller and John Schultz worked at a private high school. A seventeen year old girl's leg was cut. Mille and Schults said that "if your three sisters become Christians we affix an artificial

---

50. İsmail Taşpinar, "Bir Katolik Hiristiyan Misyon Kuruluşu Olarak Caritas Türkiye ve Günümüzde İstanbul ve Çevresindeki Faaliyetleri," *Dinler Tarihçileri Gözüyle Türkiye'de Misyonerlik,* (261-68) TÜDTAD, Ankara, 2005, p. 266.

51. Oymak et al., "Elaziğ, Tunceli ve Bingöl Çevresinde Misyonerlik Faaliyetleri," p. 130.

52. Yilmaz, "Van ve Ağri Çevresinde Misyonerlik," p. 139.

53. Taşpinar, "Bir Katolik Hiristiyan Misyon Kuruluşu Olarak Caritas Türkiye," p. 268.

leg to you and meet all of your health expenditures."[54] It is also a fact that the missionaries do not help *every* needy or poor family. They choose these people from some ethnic groups, especially from Kurds or Alawi people. The aim is to recruit these people.[55]

The eighth method is to use the originally Christian people to convert Muslims to Christianity. While in the past, domestic Christian population used to do this job, now those who migrated to foreign countries try to do this. These people had lived for a long time in the land of Ottoman State. However, because of some events such as wars and conflicts, they had to leave the land of Ottoman State and move to the European countries or America. Today, these people, mostly Armenians, come to the old places and try to convert the people living over there. These people do these activities in two ways: Either they hire a house or an apartment and begin to live there. Over time, they recognize the environment and establish good relationship with the people, they begin missionary activities, or as if they establish a society, after taking living permission and recognizing people and environment, they begin missionary activities. This method is commonly used in the eastern part of Turkey, where once these people lived for a long time.[56]

The ninth method is to give promise for the future for those who accept Christianity. This method is also very effective, especially in those areas that have great unemployment. For this purpose, they distribute some hand-

54. See Atalay, "Diyarbakir ve Mardin'de Misyonerlik Faaliyetleri," p. 161.

55. Özkan, Polat, "Erzurum, Erzincan, Kars ve Iğdir Yöresinde Misyonerlik," p. 116, 118; Şevket Yavuz, "Küreselleştirme Sürecinde Misyonerliğe Düşen Rolün Yeniden İnşasi ve Çanakkale Örneği," *Dinler Tarihçileri Gözüyle Türkiye'de Misyonerlik,* (269-79) TÜDTAD, Ankara, 2005, p. 277.

56. Yilmaz, "Van ve Ağri Çevresinde Misyonerlik," p. 135.

notice (or advertisement) that includes information about finding a job abroad. For example, a hand-notice goes as follows: "In case you apply to the following address, we will offer a job for you. This company is an international company and pays a high salary." In addition, it contains the requirements for applying a job, and a telephone number on a card for making an appointment.[57] They promise to meet all the financial needs of specially those people who want to pursue graduate studies abroad.[58]

In addition to these methods, missionaries use all kinds of means for their work. They organize some meetings for interreligious dialogue, symposiums, panels, concerts, music meeting, public rejoicings, and radio and television programmes.[59]

We may conclude this part by stating that these missionaries are not ordinary people, they possess some very special features. They try to gauge the environment where they will serve. They first come to the area and investigate whether it is inhabited by Christians. If there are some Christians or Armani people, their job is rendered easy. If not, they establish a company and hire some local people to work there. They teach these local people. They use these local people in every activity by offering them a salary. Through these local people they come to learn about the environment and try to gather some people who have weak

---

57. Oymak et al., "Elaziğ, Tunceli ve Bingöl Çevresinde Misyonerlik Faaliyetleri," p. 124.

58. Yilmaz, "Van ve Ağri Çevresinde Misyonerlik," p. 137.

59. Şinasi Gündüz, "Misyonerlerin Çalişma Yöntemleri," *Türkiye'de Misyonerlik Faaliyetleri,* (351-78) İstanbul: Ensar Neşriyat, 2005, pp. 369-76; Arslantürk, "Müzakere," pp. 391-94; M. Numan Malkoç, " İstanbul ve Çevresinde Misyonerlik," pp. 257-58; Hakki Şah Yasdiman, " İzmir, Denizli, Manisa, Uşak, Aydin ve Muğla Çevresinde Misyonerlik," *Dinler Tarihçileri Gözüyle Türkiye'de Misyonerlik,* (349-58) TÜDTAD, Ankara, 2005, p. 355 ff.

faith.[60] For this purpose, they acquire knowledge of religious and cultural features of that area. Sometimes they learn even local languages, such as Kurdish, in order to contact people easily.[61]

They are very sincere and humble people. They are very self-sacrificing. They approach people with a great esteem, regard, and love. They work by a great dynamism and organize and participate in all kinds of social activities. They use all kinds of opportunities to contact people and youth such as sport, music, and other social activities. They are very curious and interested in all kinds of things. They are very sensitive to the Muslims' values. Sometimes they wear Muslim clothes and behave like Muslims. While they give special places and importance to the youth, they show no concern for those who are above forty years old. They do not discriminate between men and women. They have various jobs and occupations. While some of them are teachers, others are doctors, pharmacists, farmers, etc.[62]

Concluding Remarks

The relationship between Muslims and Christians has continued for about a thousand years in Anatolia. For a long time, they lived in peace and harmony without intervening with each other's religion, culture and tradition. Ottoman State protected all minority groups and behaved very well towards them as long as they lived in peace. However, when Ottoman State began to decline, some minority groups began to rebel and raised problems for the Ottoman State. During this period,

---

60. Şükrü Uslu et al., "Malatya ve Adiyaman Çevresinde Misyonerlik Faaliyetleri," (165-202). *Dinler Tarihçileri Gözüyle Türkiye'de Misyonerlik*, TÜDTAD, Ankara, 2005, p. 179.

61. Yilmaz, "Van ve Ağri Çevresinde Misyonerlik," p. 139.

62 Yilmaz, "Van ve Ağri Çevresinde Misyonerlik," p. 138; Atalay, "Diyarbakir ve Mardin'de Misyonerlik Faaliyetleri," p. 148.

many foreign countries opened hundreds of schools in the land of Ottoman State. In terms of missionary activities, the nineteenth century was a golden age. During the First World War, the missionary activities lost influence by betraying the Anatolian people. As a result of their betrayal, they had to leave Turkey and most of their schools were closed. With the establishment of the Republic of Turkey, the missionary activities experienced a period of regression. However, when the Republic of Turkey passed on to the multi-party systems and followed a more democratic way, the missionary activities began to increase. When we come to our day, it is seen that the missionary activities have reached their peak levels through the adaptation of the code of laws for the European Union.[63]

In fact, nobody is disturbed by the presence of various beliefs and their followers in Turkey. Furthermore, all Muslims have great esteem towards Christianity and Judaism, for the followers of these religions are accepted as the People of the Book. Although the Qur'an invites the People of the Book to the religion of Islam,[64] it does not compel anybody to accept Islam. Thus, as long as they are sincere in their religion, and try to live according to the principles of their religion, it poses no problems for Muslims. But if they try to convert Muslims to Christianity, or try to destroy the unity of Turkish people or slander Islam and Muslims, or abuse the feelings of poor and needy people then, nobody accepts their activities. Thus, we should distinguish between the sincere Christians and missionaries. However, in the eyes of many, the missionaries are those who try to destroy the unity of Turkish people and Turkey, support the terrorists groups (for example, the

---

63. Gökbel, "Sivas ve Tokat Çevresinde Misyonerlik Faalityetleri," p. 224; Malkoç, " İstanbul ve Çevresinde Misyonerlik," pp. 252-54.

64. The Quran, 3: 64.

Armenian question), work for the interests of foreign countries and try to create new nations and new religions in Turkey.[65]

There are two basic views regarding the missionary activities in Turkey. While some people underestimate the missionary activities, others see missionary activities as a great threat for the future of Turkey and Muslim population. For example, Oymak writes that —

> As a reality and as a great danger it is an organized movement that is supported by Imperial powers. It must not be belittled. South Korea is a very nice example for us. While the Christian population was just 8-10 percent in 1950s, it has reached 60 per cent now. However, we must not exaggerate this movement too. But we must take some precautions about it.[66]

Thus, it can be said that there are two kinds of Christian activities: religious and political. Because of that the great majority of scholars and people do not accept their activities.[67]

As a result of this understanding, while some people

---

65. Küçük, "Takdim," p. 13.
66. Oymak et al., "Elaziğ, Tunceli ve Bingöl Çevresinde Misyonerlik Faaliyetleri," p. 131. See also Uslu et al., "Malatya ve Adiyaman Çevresinde Misyonerlik Faaliyetleri," pp. 201-02. As of 2004, The general situation of Christianity and Christian missionary activities is as follows: There are 70 churches in Turkey, 15 publishing houses, 11 religious foundations and associations, 9 radio broadcasting, 5 of which is found in Turkey, 4 of which is found abroad; 11 Internet websites. As to the number of people who converted to Christianity, there are different numbers. While to the official department, 339 people changed their religions since 1997, to some this number reached at 3,000. However, these numbers are not certain. See Ali Erbaş, "Müzakere," *Türkiye'de Misyonerlik Faaliyetleri,* (195-206) İstanbul: Ensar Neşriyat, 2005, p. 205.
67. Güngör, Ünal ve Adibelli, "Kayseri, Nevşehir ve Kirşehir Çevresinde Misyonerlik Faaliyetleri," p. 217.

believe that if there is a freedom of religion and a freedom of thought in Turkey and everybody has a right to believe a religion, then Christian missionaries have a right to spread their religion to those who are not Christians in this context. In the end, it is their legal right. Others assert that missionary activities are not an innocent religious movement. By contrast, their true aim is to work for the interest of the foreign countries to which they belong. In fact, they do not want to Christianize the Muslim population, they want to divide or weaken Turkey by exploiting ethnic and religious faultlines. Thus, there can be no limitless religious freedom and thought in any country in the world today. It must not contravene general morality, public order, and common good.[68]

How then should we evaluate the situation? First of all, it must be accepted that although both Islam and Christianity are missionary-oriented religions, the Islamic *da'wa* and Christian mission are very different from each other. While the Islamic *da'wa* is not an organized work, Christian mission is an organized work and it has had special people and methods designated for this purpose throughout the history.[69] As we saw above, the missionaries are special people and use all kinds of ways to evangelize the Muslim population.

When we examine the missionary activities from a legal point of view, we see that "to be respectful for Human Rights," is the basic and unchangeable principle of the Constitution.[70] In

---

68. Ali Akyildiz, "Misyonerliğe Karşi Yasal Tedbirler: Misyonerlik Bir Kamu Düzeni Sorunu mudur?" *Dinler Tarihçileri Gözüyle Türkiye'de Misyonerlik*, (399-416.) TÜDTAD, Ankara, 2005, p. 399.

69. For the definition of missionary activity and the differences between the Islamic *Da'wa* and Christian mission, see Ömer Faruk Harman, "Genel Olarak Misyonerlik," *Türkiye'de Misyonerlik Faaliyetleri*, (25-36) (İstanbul: Ensar Neşriyat, 2005), p. 29, 33.

70. See Turkish Constitution, Article 2.

addition, according to the Article 15, it is said that ". . . nobody can be forced to clarify his/her religion, thought, and conscience, and nobody can be accused because of those clarifications." However, the Turkish Constitution introduces some limitations concerning the freedom of religion and thought in some cases. According to the Article 14, nobody can use this right for undermining the unity of Turkey and her people, and for destroying Turkey as a democratic and secular Republic. Thus, Turkey has the right to protect its national safety, public safety, the basic principles of Republic and its unity. If Christian missionary activities clash with these principles, then, the state can intervene in their activities.[71]

In conclusion, I can say that both the religion of Islam and Turkish Constitution give great importance to the freedom of religion and thought. Living with various people is for Turkish people a legacy from their ancestors. People with many different faiths have lived in the land of Ottoman State in peace and prosperity for centuries. Thus, as long as people of other faiths live with harmony and peace, and do not abuse the right of freedom of religion and thought, Turkish people will always accept their presence and respect their faiths, cultures and traditions. However, if they abuse their rights, both the state and its people have the right to stop these kinds of activities, as other states do in the world today.

---

71. See more information, Akyildiz, "Misyonerliğe Karşi Yasal Tedbirler," pp. 407-11.

6

The Life of Guru Arjan Dev and its Present-day Relevance

P. S. Bhandari

THE history of the Sikhs and the history of the New World — that is to say, America, coincide. Columbus was born in 1451 and discovered America in 1492, ushering in the New Age. Vasco-da Gama was born in 1469 and discovered the sea route to India in 1498. The Old World and the New World made the world complete. This new and complete world needs a new and complete religion.

Guru Nanak the founder of Sikhism, was a contemporary of Columbus. He was born in 1469 and gave a new religion to the world, when he started preaching in 1499.

His message was based on religious harmony. He started his preaching with *Ek Oṅkār*, which means that God is one. Human race is one. There is neither Hindu nor Muslim, all are human beings, therefore respect all religions. Be a good Hindu and a good Muslim. Do not hate others. His companion, Mardānā, was a Muslim and his followers were called Sikhs, or disciples.

His other principles were: remember God, earn a living honestly and share with the needy ones. That is why there are no beggars among Sikhs. He also stood for the protection of human rights.

He preached this message of unity and harmony of all the religions and of human race throughout the world, by visiting the centres of all the great religions of the world including Mecca, Baghdad and Jerusalem.

His nine successors continued to preach this message of harmony after him. And the same message is retained in the scripture of the Sikhs — *Śrī Guru Granth Sāhib*, which was compiled by Guru Arjan Dev.

Guru Arjan is called the fifth Guru Nanak, because he was the fourth successor to the House of Guru Nanak. He was a contemporary of William Shakespeare, the great dramatist of England. He was born on 15 April 1563 and was the youngest son of Guru Ram Das Ji, the fourth Guru Nanak. He was a sportsman with a strong physique who taught painting, music, architecture, horse-riding, and the martial arts.

He was a born poet. 2,218 hymns of his are included in *Guru Granth Sāhib*.

He was chosen to the throne of Guru Nanak because of his humility, service and scholarship. He himself preached unity of all the religions and equality of all human beings through his teachings, writings and deeds.

He completed the tank of Amritsar and opened it for everybody to take bath in, as against the practice of segregation of the lower castes in other religions. He constructed the Golden Temple at Amritsar and asked a Muslim saint, Mian Mir, to lay the foundation stone of the Golden Temple. He designed the Golden Temple with four gates on all the four sides, so that anyone belonging to any caste or creed can come into the Darbar Sahib — the Golden Temple — from any side.

There is a saying that no house in the city should be taller than the Śivālaya — the Hindu temple dedicated to Śiva. So some followers suggested that the Golden Temple should also be the tallest building in the city. The Guru replied that our religion is based on humility, so it will be the lowest in the city. Humility brings peace on earth.

He compiled the Holy Bible of the Sikhism, the *Guru Granth Sāhib*. He started the Sikh scripture with *Japu Jī*, which consists of the words of Guru Nanak, the founder of Sikhism. *Japu Jī* starts with digit 1 and then *Oṅkār*. It appeals to one God, one religion and one human race. The Sikh scripture includes the hymns of only six Sikh *gurus* and of thirty non-Sikh saints. He also included therein the scriptures of the Hindu saints of low caste, who were given equality with the higher caste brāhmaṇas. He included the scriptures of the saints belonging to the different regions of India and Pakistan and internationalized it. He included the scriptures of the Muslims and thus secularized religion. Thus he made *Guru Granth Sāhib* the symbol of three harmonies: religious, racial and regional.

He included the verses of Bhagat Namdev, which imply the concept of human rights. One such verse runs: *hauṅ bhūkhe bhagat na kījey, yeh mālā āpnī lījey:* "I cannot worship You on an empty stomach, take back your rosary." Then he gives in detail what he needs: Enriched food, wife to cook, clothing, shelter and a comfortable bed. He also included the verse Begam Pura, a city in which there is no suffering, which is written by Bhagat Ravidās, an untouchable Hindu saint. *Sukhmanī Sāhib* — the psalm of peace was revealed through him. It is the most read psalm after Japjī Sāhib, the first verse of the Holy Scripture.

When he was being tortured, the same Muslim saint, Mian Mir, who laid the foundation of the Golden Temple, wanted to curse the persons who were torturing him but he asked him not to do so. Thus he put the principle of "love your enemy in action."

He was tortured to death in Lahore, which is now in Pakistan. The 400th anniversary of the martyrdom was celebrated on 16 June 2004. It was also commemorated by the Government of Pakistan in a befitting manner. The Prime Minister of Pakistan was present in person to pay him tribute. A postage stamp was issued in his memory. So was the case with the Government of India. Thus his martyrdom brought the two countries and the two religions close to each other after four hundred years.

When we explore the history of all the religions, we find all of them have been persecuted at one time or the other. Synagogues, churches, temples, mosques and gurdwaras have been demolished and burnt.

Jews have gone through the Holocaust. Christians were persecuted even by the Christians themselves. The Holy prophet Mohammed had to leave Mecca and his followers were persecuted. Hindus went through hell of a time for almost 800 years. Sikhs went through two holocausts and were hunted like wild beasts.

Before 9/11, the Sikhs were trying to prove that the Sikhism was not Hinduism. After 9/11, the Sikhs are trying to prove that they are not Muslims because of their similar appearance. The Sikhs experience a threefold hatred: first, because they are Sikhs; second, because they look like Muslims; and third, because they are non-Whites. Now every religion is at war against other religions.

The history demonstrates that religions tend to flourish as a result of being persecuted. Dr Mohammed Iqbal writes: *īmāna ẓindā hotā hai, har karbalā key bād.* (Religion revives after every tragedy). When the Sikhs were being annihilated, a saying sprang up:

mannu sāḍi datri, asien mannu dey soye,
jyoṅ jyoṅ sanūṅ vaḍhdā,
asieṅ tyoṅ tyoṅ dūney hoye.

> Mannu, a tyrant of a ruler, is our sickle and we are like grass. As he cuts us, we grow double.

So the Religion will come out with flying colours after 9/11. Some good things have already been started. It is time to remember his famous teachings to find out a solution of terrorism of these days:

> Since I received the company of the saints
> The sense of estrangement is vanished.
> Foe and stranger there is none
> I am at peace with everyone.

The tenth Nanak put his seal also on this sentiment as follows: *manus kī jātī sabai ek hi pehchabo*. That is to say: Consider all human race as one. (The differences are because of different geographical conditions.)

Guru Arjan further says:

> Thy will is sweet. If we surrender before the will of God, keep the company of the saintly persons, colour ourselves in spirituality, do not hate others, and treat them as equals, then all the religions will flourish and there will be peace on earth.

7

Mira Behn : An Environmentalist of the Himalayas

George James

AMONG the many political, diplomatic, economic, and social issues that have come to public attention in the light of the events of 11 September 2001, environmental issues have been less than prominent. Yet threats to the environment in many parts of the world can hardly be divorced from the availability of petroleum resources that are needed for the exploitation of other natural resources and for industrial development. Recognition of the vulnerability of these resources to political and paramilitary threats has led some to consider an assessment of the resources that remain on the earth and to consider appropriate measures for their prudent use and conservation, as well as alternative strategies for the production of the needed energy.

There is perhaps no land mass on the earth that has been more continuously occupied or more effectively utilized for the production of the means for human survival than India. For millennia, and by a great variety of means, India had managed scarce resources to feed, clothe, and shelter an enormous and enormously diverse population. These means for survival were marginalized by colonialism as her forest resources came to be regarded as among her most valuable disposable assets. During this period, her population was also seen as a ready market for colonialism's material products. The movement for Independence, as Gandhi conceived of it, was a movement towards the re-establishment of sustainable village level industries that colonialism had undermined. His view was that the heart of India, her villages, had to be economically independent if she was to realize political independence as a nation.

In India, today, there are few persons more associated with environmentalism than Sunderlal Bahuguna. From the time of the famous "Chipko Andolan," he has drawn public attention to the condition of India's environment by means of *satyāgraha*s against contract felling of the Himalayan forests, against big dams that displace large numbers of productive and hard working people, and against the religion of economics that enriches the few at the expense of the many. Bahuguna acknowledges that his interest in the environment and his inspiration for its preservation came from an encounter with one of Gandhi's most famous English disciples, who went to live in the Garhwal hills after Gandhi's assassination.[1] Her story can be seen as the development of an environmentalist, inspired and informed by Gandhi's concern for the establishment of independent and self-reliant villages.

Born in 1927, Sunderlal Bahuguna had joined the Independence struggle at the age of 13. At 17 he was jailed for his role in transmitting information concerning Sri Dev Suman's imprisonment in Tehri, to the nationalist press in Delhi. With the help of a physician who treated him for afflictions he acquired in the unsanitary conditions of the jail, he escaped the clutches of the jailers to a remote region of Punjab where for a year he lived underground. Following that year he completed his university education in Lahore.

1. Sunderlal Bahuguna, "Fount of Motherly Love," in Krishna Murthi Gupta, *Mira Behn, Gandhiji's Daughter Disciple: Birth Centenary Volume* (New Delhi: Himalaya Seva Sangh, 1992), p. 251.

When Independence came to India, Bahuguna returned to the Tehri Garhwal region, and was appointed general secretary of the Prajamandal, the Congress committee for the region. But in the course of eight years he came to doubt the capacity of party politics to address the economic condition of the hills and committed himself to Gandhi's constructive programme for local communities. It was in the context of his involvement with Gandhi's constructive programme that he came to know Mira Behn. She had come to the Garhwal hills after an extended association with Gandhi. But her interest in nature that flourished in the Garhwal hills had its roots in her early life in England. Born in London in 1892, the woman known to India as Mira Behn was the daughter of a British naval officer, Sir Edmond Slade, later Admiral Slade, Commander-in-Chief of the British East Indies Fleet. She was known then as Madeline Slade. Her coming to India, her discipleship to Gandhi, and her constructive work in the hills seems almost to have been foreshadowed in her childhood. In her autobiography she states that, as early as the age of five or six, there was something that every now and again, as she put it, "wafted me far away." Always provoked by the voice of nature, the song of a bird, or the sound of the wind in the trees, the experience engendered, she says, "an infinite joy." At this stage she began to search in what she calls the region of "the unknowable."[2] During her father's long absences, she experienced a deep sense of fellowship with the trees, plants, and animals in the twenty acres of her grandfather's country home. She states that there were some trees for which she had a special affection, but that all were personalities. She states, "I can remember throwing my arms around the trees and embracing them."[3]

---

2. Mira Behn, *The Spirit's Pilgrimage* (Arlington VA: Great Ocean Publishers, 1960), pp. 20-21.

3. Mira Behn, p. 12.

Her childhood rapport with nature was supported by an intense devotion to music. It was music, in fact, that led her, through a circuitous route, to Gandhi. She states that at age of 15, when she encountered it for the first time, the music of Beethoven illuminated her spirit. Exploring the life of Beethoven, she found that nature had been the inspiration for much of his music. She also learned that Beethoven had copied long passages from German translations of Sanskrit literature, and that it had touched him profoundly.[4] Her pursuit of the music of Beethoven led her at age 30 to Switzerland to visit his biographer, the Nobel Laureate, Romain Rolland. On meeting him, she found that Rolland was also deeply interested in contemporary events in India and especially in the ideas and activities of Gandhi. He asked her whether she had ever heard of Gandhi. When she replied that she had not, he talked to her about him, comparing his character to that of Christ.[5] His words made such an impression that the conversation remained in her mind through her travels to Egypt. On her return, she visited Paris where she bought Rolland's new book on Gandhi, and read it in a single day. Then she immersed herself in Gandhi's own writings and felt she had found there, at last, the meaning of her life. Before she arrived home in England, she was convinced that she was called to go to India, to stand with Gandhi in his commitment to truth and non-violence in the cause of India's freedom.

After corresponding with Gandhi and a period of disciplined preparation, she sailed for Bombay on 25 October 1925, arriving on 6 November. Colleagues of Gandhi were there to receive her. Without delay she boarded an overnight train to Ahmedabad and from there went by car to the

---

4. Mira Behn, "Autobiographical Note" in Krishna Murthi Gupta, op. cit., p. 295; Mira Behn, *Gandhiji's Daughter Disciple: Birth Centenary Volume*, p. 295.
5. Mira Behn, p. 58.

Sabarmati Āśram, where her eyes finally came to rest upon the man whose ideals she had now made her own. She testifies that she was conscious of nothing but a sense of light. She fell to her knees. Raising her up with gentle hands, his first words to her were that she would be his daughter.[6] He gave her the name Mira Behn, after Mīrā of Rajasthan, the renowned devotee of Kṛṣṇa; Behn meant sister. Mira quickly became an active participant in the life of the Āśram. Shedding the habits of her privileged life, she arose with others at 4:00 a.m. and attended morning prayers at 4:30 a.m. She took part in sweeping and cleaning the Āśram, including the cleaning of the latrines. Having taken up spinning in her preparation to be with Gandhi, she now learned the art of carding cotton and other activities related to *khādī*, the industry of making home-made cloth. With others she took her turn in the kitchen, where *dāl, roṭī*s and vegetables were prepared daily for 200 people.[7] In a short time, she became an Indian both in her food habits and in her manner of dress. It was in this period, and after a long discussion with Gandhi, that she chose to shave her hair and take the vow of celibacy. She journeyed first to Delhi to learn Hindi and then to Hardwar. Then after further training in carding, spinning, and weaving she began to accompany Gandhi on his *khādī* tours, the journeys in which he instilled among the villagers the importance of village independence through the revival of village industries, village government, village sanitation, and village education, now including the education of women.

For her discipleship to Gandhi, Mira Behn spent two extended periods in prison, during which time she immersed herself in the religious literature of India. On Gandhi's

---

6. Krishna Murthi Gupta, op. cit., pp. 4-6. See also http://www.mkgandhi.org/associates/Mirabehn.htm

7. Mira Behn, "How Bapuji Trained his Followers," in Gupta, pp. 285-86.

recommendation she read the *Mahābhārata* and the *Rāmāyaṇa*, the two great epics of the Hindu tradition. Later, he recommended readings from the eleven principal Upaniṣads, and selections from the Vedas. Of these writings she said: "I discovered things that seemed to be part of my inmost self, part of something I had known long before and since lost." About her encounter with the Vedas she tells us: "I heard the same note as in the music of Beethoven, and my heart stirred and then hushed again as if waiting for a later time."[8] During her second period in prison, she witnessed the death of Gandhi's wife, Kasturba Gandhi and Mahadev Desai, his right hand man. From this time, Mira Behn began to work more independently of Gandhi, and it was in this period that her interest in environmental issues began to take shape. She began now to recover the sense of communion with nature that had been curtailed during the strenuous years in the struggle for political independence.

The environmentalism that now emerges in her life was expressed in three related ways. One was a clear personal religious sense of devotion to nature. Another was a succession of efforts to establish communities in which human beings could live in harmony and communion with nature. Third was her many writings in support of nature and against its exploitation and abuse. To treat them in historical order, I shall start with the second. In 1947 she established an *āśram* called Pashulok, near Rishikesh. She intended that Pashulok, meaning animal world, would be a centre in which human beings could work in harmony with nature to promote human development according to Gandhi's ideals.[9] In a letter, Gandhi expressed approval of the concept and the name. It was not an unmitigated success. While government help for such projects was now available, Mira Behn found that the emerging

8. Mirabehn, pp. 170-71.

9. Gupta, p. 24.

bureaucracy stood in the way of her purpose. She decided to start a registered organization called the Pashulok Seva Mandal as an alternative. Its purpose, as she conceived of it, was "to develop an area or areas where men and animals combine with nature in the formation of a decentralized society demonstrative of Bapu's ideals for World Peace, where man in his own village will, along with his cattle, be self-sufficient, healthy and happy."[10] But neither was this a complete success. Financial support gradually waned. She decided to return the land for Pashulok to the government of Uttar Pradesh, and began to look elsewhere for a place to realize these ideals.[11] She found such a place near the village of Geonli nearly 28 miles from Tehri, a scenic region replete with thick pine forests and a clear view of several glaciers. The forest department leased her two acres of land. She called it Gopal Āśram, taking the name from Lord Kṛṣṇa in his role as cowherd.[12]

The personal significance of nature for Mira Behn is no more clearly expressed than the meaning she found in nature in one of her darkest hours. With the news of Gandhi's assassination on 30 January 1948, Mira Behn was struck with grief. Friends came to her to make arrangements for her to go to Delhi. But she remembered Gandhi's words to her that the spirit she loves is always with her. And she remembered his admonition to "trust God and be where you are." She decided not to go. She made a visit to Delhi near the end of February that year. She visited the site of his assassination and the cremation ground at Rajghat, but she found no solace there for her grief, and there she cried to herself: "Let me go back to the life and light of the fields and forests, where nature

10. Ibid., p. 33.
11. Ibid., p. 34.
12. Mira Behn, p. 302.

knows no such thing as mourning for the dead, because in her there is no death. For me Bapu is there, not here."[13] Later, when she declined to be present at the immersion of Gandhi's ashes at the confluence of the Gaṅgā and Yamunā Rivers, his friends sent a portion of his ashes for her to immerse in the Gaṅgā at Rishikesh. She states that as she walked to the *ghāṭ* with the little urn of his ashes in her hand, she lost any feeling of her body and did not so much as sense the ground beneath her naked feet. She writes,

> Gaṅgā's pure and sparkling water was swirling by the wooden platform that had been built out over the stream. As I cast the ashes into the swift blue current I felt, as never before, the glory of nature who takes our earthly remains back to her bosom in all-embracing love.[14]

Bahuguna's first encounter with Mira Behn began when she was residing at Pashulok near Rishikesh. She was travelling by horse into the hills to find the place that would become the Gopal Āśram. In her travels she had come to Tehri, where Sunderlal was now general secretary of the Congress Committee. Having heard of her work with Gandhi, and knowing that she was committed to Gandhi's ideals, Sunderlal went to see her. He explains that, because she was a woman of the ruling class, she was accommodated in a large bungalow provided for guests of the state. But when he reached her room he found her sitting on the floor, spinning at a portable Charkha. Sunderlal points out that Gandhians are always eager to encourage younger workers. Politics, he says, makes little room for such new blood. But the Gandhians are always eager to train new workers, and provide them with knowledge and opportunity for service. She immediately took an interest in Sunderlal because, as he put it, he was a youngster of 21.

13. Ibid., p. 296. Cited by Gupta, p. 32.
14. Ibid., 295. Cited by Gupta p. 33.

Having lived in India from age 33, Mira Behn was now 56. To Sunderlal, she was the embodiment of Gandhian ideals. She had assimilated the essence of Indian life as expressed in its philosophy and its religion. "Our religion," he says, "teaches us respect for all forms of life." Following their initial conversation, she invited Sunderlal to her āśram near Rishikesh which he then began to visit on a regular basis.

With Independence, economic development had now become a national priority. Mira Behn observed that "huge industrial and other projects were being planned, for which gigantic sums of money had to be borrowed, or accepted as gifts from other countries." She saw this as something completely different from what Gandhi had pictured for a free India.[15] In an article in *Harijan* in 1949 called "Development or Destruction" and a follow-up article entitled "Startling Facts," she points out that much of what has been called development has come at the cost of grasslands that had once been grazing land for cattle. She argues that the true development of such lands would have included the introduction of more appropriate species of grasses and the cultivation of fodder crops.[16] She drew attention to the danger in the proliferation of large irrigation systems that led to water-logging and soil alkalinity and had by then resulted in thousands of acres of once productive land going out of cultivation. She pointed out that crops nourished with artificial fertilizers are inferior in quality to those nourished with compost, and argued that vegetables and fodder grown with artificial fertilizers are actually harmful to men and beasts. She pointed out that sugar cane "occupies the land on which it is grown for a period long enough for growing two to three grain crops." She argued that more appropriate and

15. Ibid., p. 306.
16. Gupta, p. 141.

wholesome sources of sugar are the palm trees that grow freely on land unsuited for cultivation.[17] Mother Earth, she argues, does her best to feed us all. We, therefore, ought to serve her as dutiful children.[18] Much of what is being called development, she says, is nothing but destruction.[19]

With the establishment of Gopal Āśram, she began a monthly publication called *Bapu Raj Patrika*. The journal was produced in English and Hindi as well as Gujarati, Tamil, and Telugu. It was addressed in very simple language to the peasantry of India. Her objective, as she puts it, "was to try to explain to the villagers the kind of self-reliant economy that Bapu had visualized for them, and to urge them to get together in a common demand for a simple decentralized society."[20] Bahuguna assisted her in the production of the Hindi translation of this publication.[21]

While publishing the journal she travelled by horse from one village to another, meeting farmers' groups and addressing local communities. Yet her days at Gopal Āśram were also full of activity, and they always began with the cows. J.P. Uniyal, who worked during these days as her secretary, reports that Mira Behn was an ardent votary of ecological balance, organic farming, shallow ploughing, and the use of compost and earth worms for preserving humus, and that she carried on a sustained correspondence on these subjects with kindred spirits in the West, chiefly among the Quakers.[22] In his own reminiscence Bahuguna points out that her love of animals even extended to the rats of the fields and on one

17. Ibid., pp. 144-45.
18. Ibid., p. 137.
19. Ibid., p. 141.
20. Mira Behn, p. 306. Cited by Gupta, p. 36.
21. Gupta, pp. 35-36.
22. J.P. Uniyal, "Memories of Mira Behn," in Gupta, pp. 253-54.

occasion to a leopard. He relates that on one occasion, when he visited the Gopal Āśram to help with the publication of *Bapu Raj Patrika,* he was working with others in a maize field, when they saw a rat emerging from a hole. Their first impulse was to find a cat to kill it. But when they returned with the cat, they found Mira Behn feeding roasted maize to the rat, while birds were congregating to feed on raisins. He relates that another time a leopard was haunting the area. The villagers told her that the leopard was killing their cows and had to be trapped and killed. In accord with the strategy of the hills, they fashioned a trap with a live goat as bait. In the morning they were pleased to find the trap was shut, but disappointed to find only the goat in the trap. Mira Behn told the people that she could not sleep knowing that we were intending to catch the leopard by means of such a trick. She explained that in the night she had gotten up and shut the trap herself.

In addition to *Bapu Raj Patrika,* Mira Behn wrote extensively for publications like *Young India* and *Harijan,* as well as for newspapers such as the *Hindustan Times* and *The Statesman.* It was here that she expressed some of her most critical ecological concerns. In an article in the *Hindustan Times* in 1950 she announced, "There is something radically wrong in the Himalayas, and that "something" is, without doubt, connected with the forests." The problem, she said, is not simply that the hills are being denuded but that there has been a gradual but significant shift in the species of trees that cover these hills. The change which she had observed over time had been from the Himalayan Oak, called Banj, to the Chir Pine. This change had been allowed to proceed, she says, because the Oak forests provide no revenue to the government while the Chir Pine is profitable, providing revenue both from timber and resin for turpentine. She argues, however, that the profit from the timber and resin of the Chir Pine is hardly equal to the damage that occurs from floods as a result of the loss of the Oak.

> The Banj leaves, falling as they do, year by year, create a rich black mould in which develops a thick tangled mass of undergrowth (bushes, creepers, and grasses), which in their turn add to the leaf-mould deposit and the final result is a forest in which almost all the rain water gets absorbed. Some of it evaporates back into the air and the rest percolates slowly down to the lower altitudes, giving out here and there beautiful sweet and cool springs. It would be difficult to imagine a more ideal shock-absorber for the monsoon rains than a Banj forest.

She explains that the Chir pine produces only a dry carpet of needles that absorbs nothing and prevents the development of significant undergrowth.

> When the torrential rains of the monsoon beat down on these southern slopes of the Himalayas, much of the pine-needle carpet gets washed away with the water and erosion invariably takes place, because these needles, being non-absorbent, create no leaf-mould, but only a little inferior soil, which is easily washed out from the rocks and stones.[23]

For Mira Behn, the Banj forests are the centre of nature's economic cycle on the southern slopes of the Himalayas. To consent to their destruction, she argues, is to cut out the heart of the whole natural system. Constructive workers, she said, should organize village committees and village guards to work along with the Forest Department to protect and maintain the forests. By such means she envisioned a long-term project to control the lopping of the trees and a gradual recovery of the Banj forests. "The forests of the Himalayas," she says, "are the guardians of the Northern Plains, which, in their turn, are

---

23. "Something Wrong in the Himalayas," in Gupta, p. 145.

the Granary of India. Surely such guardians deserve the utmost care and attention that the Government can give them."[24]

Bahuguna came quickly to understand the gravity of these ecological issues. But her hopes for a sustainable community in which human beings and nature could exist harmoniously together were never fulfilled. With little money left and her hopes for Pashulok, Gopal Āśram, and other efforts unfulfilled, she retired to a picturesque place in the Garhwal Hills near Chamba. She called it Pakshi Kunj, meaning the grove of birds. There she wrote her memoirs, and there she began to recall the music that had moved her so many years before. Recognizing that the heat and malaria of the plains and the steep terrain of the hills was a severe challenge to her health, she finally decided to return to Europe. She went first to England and then to Vienna where she continued to campaign through her writings and lectures for the preservation of the Himalayan environment, and the propagation of Gandhi's ideas.

Though she departed from India in 1959, the impact of her life upon the people of the hills still continues. There is perhaps no single life upon whom this impact was more pronounced than that of Sunderlal Bahuguna. He described her influence as forming the foundation of his thought. Following her departure Bahuguna continued to organize community groups at the grass-roots towards the common demand for the simple, decentralized, and sustainable society that Gandhi had envisioned and that Mira Behn had tried to realize. One of the most important long-term results of her work in the hills was the organization of labour co-operatives that eventually contributed to the emergence of a movement of the people in the 1970s known as Chipko. In 1981 his

---

24. Ibid., pp. 146-47.

involvement with this movement brought Bahuguna to Europe, and to Vienna where at last he met Mira Behn again. She was pleased to hear that her call to save the mountains was now being voiced by the people. He told her: "When you tried to awaken us, we still continued to sleep. Now we are active and you are so very far away." In reply she said to him, "Go to nature. She will restore the Himalayas to its original glory."[25] Mira Behn died in Vienna on 20 July 1982. She will be remembered by those she touched as one of the most important inspirations for environmental movements in India that continue to work towards village economic self-reliance.

25. Sunderlal Bahuguna, "Fount of Motherly Love" in Gupta, p. 252.

8

How Australian Indigenous Women Transform Christianity

Lee Miena Skye

I AM a Tasmanian Aboriginal (a *Palawa*) descended from the last "full blood" before the genocide. It was one of the swiftest acts of genocide in the history of humanity. There are about 5,000 of us left with blood-linkage, and there are those of us who keep the culture and language alive. Tasmanian aboriginals were a very gentle people which is why we were able to be brought into genocide so quickly. I was brought up in the stories of the atrocities and have had a hatred of racism ever since. I have a zero tolerance to all forms of violence. Destiny would have it that I became a womanist (black feminist) theologian,[1] writing out of this universal academic tradition against the forms of violence that our women suffer, racism (conscious and subconscious), classism, sexism (including heterosexism) and to which I add naturism (abuse of nature). White feminist theology, in comparison, deals mainly with the single-issue oppression of sexism and its affects on all dimensions of existence.[2]

1. This is a historical event for our women in that Australian aboriginal women's religion has never been represented at the parliament in history.

2. See Lee Skye, "An investigation into Black feminine/feminist Christology/theology in comparison to White feminine/feminist Christology/theology," in *Tiddas Talking Business*, ed. A. Pattel-Gray, ISPCK, Voices from the Edge Series No. 1, Delhi, 2000, ch.8.

Just like my ancestral grandmother, Fanny Cochrane Smith, the last "full blood," I found strength to cope with multi-dimensional oppression through the inculturation of Christianity into my indigenous spirituality. Fanny was very proud of her culture and believed strongly that it was God's will to be so. On the 300 acres (the white man was given an average of 3,000 acres) granted to her by the government for being the only remaining aboriginal, on which I lived for most of my childhood, she had a Methodist church built and preached in it in 1898. She did not care that it was unheard of for women to do so, she understood the love and support of a God who had helped her survive the horror of seeing her whole race brought into genocide before her very eyes. A God that comes to the least in the times of their greatest suffering. It was this God she preached. Her church was the first I entered into and began my destiny to follow in her footsteps.

The Development of My Scholarship

It was a kidney operation that brought me to a state where I could not do much else but read, and consequently discovered womanist theology, I was amazed to see that I thought like these women, and my experiences were so similar, so I began to write and was encouraged to publish. I gathered degrees in the process and my Masters research thesis produced the first Australian Indigenous womanist Christology in academic history.[3] I understood that it was my ancestral grandmother's belief system that had helped her survive the effects of genocide, and that this was also the case for the mainland indigenous women who are entering into genocide. Their belief systems must be powerful indeed, and, as my research has

3. Lee Miena Skye, "*Kerygmatics* of the New Millennium: A Study of Australian Aboriginal Women's Christology," MA thesis, University of South Australia, Adelaide, South Australia, 1998 (in press) ISPCK publications, New York and Delhi, 2006/7.

proven, make a unique and very substantial contribution to Christian theology. The theology of the least is indeed the most powerful theology.

The Masters thesis was the basis for my PhD research thesis where I documented for the first time in academic history the women's soteriology, ecclesiology, eschatology, pneumatology, theology and creation theology.[4] In the PhD thesis I have explored and proven a second hypothesis that "racial ontology is carried in the genes." Again its foundation was as an intuitive understanding documented in the Masters thesis but in the PhD thesis I was able to take it several stages further, for it to become confirmed academic knowledge. My people were more white-skinned than dark-skinned yet they have the same social problems per capita as the mainland indigenous peoples. To me the problem was more than skin deep, my intuition told me that it was ontological, as I define it (way of being in the world). Australian aboriginal peoples have an extremely spiritual ontology, while white Western ontology can be described as very intellectual/cerebral. It makes it very difficult for white people to understand the way we function, our ontology, the way I see it, helping to cause the failure of assimilation policies in the past. In the present this ontological difference is at the base of our inability to fit comfortably into white Western culture. I was able to prove through various biological/psychological studies done in the USA and Japan that "spirituality can be carried in the genes," and thus, racial ontology can be carried in the genes.[5] This gave answers to what I already knew intuitively.

---

4. Lee Miena Skye, "*Yiminga* (Spirit) Calling: A Study of Australian Aboriginal Christian Women's Creation Theology," PhD thesis, University of Sydney, Sydney, NSW, Australia, 2004 (forthcoming).

5. See "Set the Spirit Free: The Need for an Australian Aboriginal Christian Womanist Research Methodology," in Skye, *Yiminga* (Spirit) Calling. PhD thesis, ch. 2.

Understanding Australian Aboriginal Christian Women's Theology

To understand the women's theology you must be able to comprehend their ontology. They are extremely spiritual women which makes them powerful theists. For field research for the PhD thesis, I lived and hunted with the traditional Christian women in central and northern Australia and south-east South Australia for approximately a year in order to understand their ontology in depth. They relate to God out of their spirits not doctrine. It is the inculturation of Christian doctrine into their indigenous spiritualities. This has produced definite indigenous Christian doctrines that contribute to and challenge white Western Christian theology, and help to lay the foundation in, what I call, the new academic area of Indigenous Christian theology/spirituality. For the first time in history these women are no longer silent, considered insignificant; they show that they have a unique and dynamic contribution to make to the academic discipline of Christian theology.

How the Women Transform Christianity

A spiritual, theistic attitude towards Christianity makes them spiritual theologians. The inculturation of Christianity into their indigenous spiritualities, after the data analysis, has revealed several main themes that naturally emerge. Firstly, God "is," there is no doubt in the existence of God. Secondly, the "interconnectedness" of all things. God's spirit is in all things (all of nature, human and non-human), therefore, all of Creation is sacralized. Thus, the "sacredness" of Creation is fundamental to their beliefs. Hence, their theologies are "Creation-centred." Christ, therefore, becomes one with Creation, transformed from fall/redemption centredness to Creation-centredness. He, in Tiwi language, is the Yiminga (Spirit) of Christianity, and of the Tiwi Islander people, He is the "pulse and breath of life." Thus, He is their very breath, and their "everything." They need him to be their everything to survive multi-dimensional oppression or what I call "quadri-dimensional" oppression.

These themes run through all their indigenous Christian doctrines that emerge from the data analysis. Thus, Christ and Christianity are transformed by ontology, indigenous spiritualities and Weltanschauungen (world-views) forming out of ontology, and their Sitze im Leben (life-settings), political, social and the natural environment.

Conclusion

Our women belong to a race that is fast approaching genocide. They are surviving quadri-dimensional through the inculturation of Christianity into their aboriginal spiritualities, and uplifting their communities in the process. They were and still are experiencing tremendous levels of mental, physical, spiritual and verbal abuse, their health is often compromised, but they find strength in their belief systems to not be perpetuators of abuse but through grace and intelligence to bring as much healing and peace to their communities as they are able.

There are psychologists and clinical psychologists in Australia fascinated that there are belief systems that are helping indigenous people survive their "holocaust." My ancestral grandmother witnessed the total genocide of her people before her eyes and found strength in her inculturated Christianity to cope with this trauma. This brings hope to those in the world suffering the threat of genocide. Hope to those caught up in the September 11 tragedy, and persistent threats.

It has been an honour for me to represent the voices of our women for the first time in the history of the Congress, and an honour to bring their message of hope for those experiencing the violence of mankind's inhumanity. The women are so thrilled that they may be able to encourage other people at this time.

9

Of Terror and Tranquillity : The Ramaṇāśrama – A Gendered Perspective

Vijaya Ramaswamy

11 SEPTEMBER 2001 has been one of the blackest days in the history of humanity. What can an act of terror which destroyed so many innocent lives have to do with the Ramaṇāśrama, a remote hermitage tucked away amidst the soft reddish mountains of Tiruvannamalai in Tamil Nadu?

The answer to this question lies at the root of the quest of a world that has turned to spirituality in these moments of emotional crisis and social insecurity caused by terror. Following the attack on the twin towers in New York which destroyed hundreds of lives, shocked devotees of Ramaṇāśrama the world over, wrote back to their spiritual home in Tiruvannamalai — seeking solace, seeking answers to the why and how of the 9/11 tragedy. This paper is built around some of the responses they received. These responses were not answers except for the reference to *prārabdha* or *karma* which is an explanation rather than an answer. The responses however provided striking insights into what ails our societies and what could be its antidote.

A hermitage without an established order of ascetics; followers without a *guru*; a renunciate who belongs to no ascetic order — this could be a factual description of the Ramaṇāśrama in Tiruvannamalai. Yet the Ramaṇāśrama has been a vibrant centre of spiritual living cutting across race, class, caste and gender for over a hundred years now. It is also a focal point for multi-faith dialogue with a following drawn not only from Hindus but from Christians, Parsis and Muslims as well, living in any part of our globe. Ramaṇa's unique philosophy of "**Who am I**" shattered ethnic and social boundaries associated with the physical body and looked beyond the gross form into the metaphysical essence of "I." The search for one's **R**eal **S**elf in contradistinction to the false **s**elf which is name and form specific, ends when the self is perceived to be the universal **"I."** Ramaṇa's philosophy, which marked a surgical break with orthodox streams of Hindu philosophy, opened the floodgates for the creation of a unique cultural mosaic in which stereotypes became meaningless. This article will focus on the women — Indians and foreigners — who discovered their spiritual space and self-expression in the Ramaṇāśrama. This work is intended to be an act of academic activism responding to the crying need for ethnic and cultural harmony in the present times.

The reigning spirit in the *āśrama* even today is still the vivid spiritual presence of Ramaṇa. On 14 April 1950, Srī Ramaṇa Bhagavān took mahāsamādhi. Forty-five years since that day, women devotees continue to live, work and meditate in the Ramaṇāśrama. Women, especially destitutes, widows and spiritual aspirants flocked to the Ramaṇāśrama, during Ramaṇa's time as well as after 1950 when his physical presence was lost to his devotees. The number of devotees, both Indian and foreign who have made the Ramaṇāśrama their sole refuge or second home, is so great that it is not possible to offer a narration of their lives and contact with Bhagavān Ramaṇa. Hence I shall confine myself to a detailed account of the life, works and experiences of those women, both Indian and foreign who were direct devotees (note: not disciples) of Ramaṇa. Those women devotees, who have been drawn to

Ramaṇāśrama after 1950 by their own insurmountable afflictions and/or the spiritual presence of Ramaṇa, will be quoted only to establish terms of reference.

The spiritual women of Ramaṇāśrama have to be situated in terms of Ramaṇa's own philosophy which had a tendency to shatter all doctrines and break all conventions. The path of self-enquiry, the eternal enquiry into the "I" rendered unnecessary the orthodox paths of ritual, prayer and monasticism. It is important to note that Ramaṇa founded no monastic order and Ramaṇāśrama, despite its name, *āśrama* is not a conventional hermitage. This is also perhaps one of the main reasons why women have gained entry into it in such large numbers. Secondly, Ramaṇa himself was not an ordained *saṁnyāsī*. He never wore the ochre robe which is conferred on a man (not woman) at the time of his formal initiation into an ascetic order. At the time of initiation even the original name of the initiate is replaced with a name specific to that order. But Ramaṇa had no *guru* and no formal initiation into *saṁnyāsa*. He retained his own name "Venkata Ramaṇan" till his last days except that he gained world renown under the name "Ramaṇa Maharṣi," a name bestowed upon him by Kavya Kanta Ganapati Muni. The absence of an established monastic order with the concomitant ritual of ascetic initiation encouraged women to gravitate towards Ramaṇa and the Ramaṇāśrama.

I got a curious proof of the universal appeal of Ramaṇa in 1994 when I went to the *āśrama.*[1] A Spanish lady called Louisa (of Peru in Latin America) living in Australia, narrated to me the following incident. In 1980 she happened to visit her friend living in Sydney. In the friend's house she came across a picture

1. The word *āśrama* can be literally translated as "hermitage," but the two are substantially different in that the *āśrama* is more loosely used and goes beyond any formal monastic structure. I have therefore preferred the use of this Sanskrit term in this article.

of Bhagavān Ramaṇa whom of course she did not recognize. She however found a lurking smile on Ramaṇa's face and told her friend, "Look, he is smiling at me." The friend told her about Ramaṇa and the Ramaṇāśrama of which she was a staunch devotee. Louisa went again and again to stare at the indescribably beautiful face of Ramaṇa. One day her friend showed her another small picture of Bhagavān, which she worshipped. When Louisa touched the picture she had the electrifying effect of being hit hard on the side (chest?). Completely taken aback, she told her friend: "He hit me!" Later she begged her friend for the picture who directed her instead to a book-store for spiritual literature. This was the beginning of her romance with Ramaṇa. Louisa said that she could experience within herself, without much difficulty, Ramaṇa's extremely difficult philosophy summed up in the words "who am I?" It was thus that Louisa stood within the precincts of the Ramaṇāśrama in 1994 when I met her. Walle Philippe Nicole, a French citizen who comes from the West Indies, is dark skinned and says that her great-grandfather was one Swaminathan from Tanjavūr. Bhagavān appeared in a vision and told her "Don't go here and there. Live in peace in Tiruvannamalai." Women like Louisa and Nicole, both Indians and foreigners, have today made Ramaṇāśrama their refuge, their home, their hermitage.

Lucy Carnelssen, whom the āśramites called "Lucy Ma" and who passed away only recently, wrote one of the most powerful expositions of Bhagavān's philosophy called *Hunting the I*. Lucy describes the uniqueness of Aruṇāchala where the Ramaṇāśrama is located:

> There is a certain mountain belonging to the Eastern Ghats about 200 km south-west of Madras named Aruṇāchala meaning "Hill of fire" or "Hill of Dawn." The Puranas claim that it is the most ancient mountain on earth. Folklore, legend, fairy tale? Well, geographical research has confirmed the "fairy tale." It is generally agreed nowadays that

> originally the Deccan was not a part of the main body of Asia but represents the remnant of a continent now lost in the depths of the ocean stretching out over Malaysia to Sumatra, Borneo, Java, Celebes and the Philippines. The Himalayas are said to have risen only in a later period. . . .[2]

Ramaṇa, the divine sage of Aruṇāchala, was a self-realized being whose luminous presence not only cured the afflicted but also showed them the path of spirituality. Brihadambal, now aged 85, told me about the women of Ramaṇāśrama: "All those who come here are "amaṅgalī" (women who are widowed) and not "sumaṅgalī" (women whose husbands are alive)." Brihadambal herself had been widowed soon after attaining maturity and came to the *āśrama* as a young widow of twenty. Her aunt Shantammal, also a widow, was already serving in Bhagavān Ramaṇa's kitchen. Brihadambal's statement to a large extent defines the social status of the Ramaṇāśrama women. Here these women not only found shelter but social respectability and acceptability and above all the path to salvation. If true feminism lies not in clamouring for gender equality (born out of a masculinity complex) but in accepting the femaleness of the woman, then Ramaṇa's philosophy restored women's identity and self-esteem in his very act of recognition that women are different and equal.

It is then important to introduce this account of women in the Ramaṇāśrama with Ramaṇa's strong views on woman's right to spirituality, asceticism and salvation. Ramaṇa's exposition was in response to a question from Visalakshi Ammal, the wife of the renowned Kavyakanta Ganapati Shastri. She had asked Ramaṇa:

1. If obstacles confront women that abide in the self, does the Śāstra (Hindu canon) sanction their renouncing the home and becoming ascetics?

---

2. Cornelssen 1970: 2.

2. If a woman, liberated while alive, happens to shed her body, what is the proper thing to do, cremation or burial?

Ramaṇa gave his decision in the following terms. First, since there is no such prohibition in the Śāstras, there is nothing wrong in women abiding in the self and when fully ripe spiritually, becoming ascetics. Second, as in *mukti* (liberation) and *jñāna* (self-knowledge) there is no difference between man and woman, the body of a woman who had become liberated during her lifetime, is not to be cremated for it is a temple. Therefore evils that are said to follow the cremation of the body of a man, who had attained liberation, will follow even when the body is that of a self-liberated woman (*jīvan-mukta*).

Kavya Kanta Ganapati sums up in poetry, Ramaṇa's arguments on female salvation and asceticism in the thirteenth chapter of his *Ramaṇa Gītā*. He says:

1. In saṁnyāsa the equal right of women and men is authenticated.
2. As there are no restrictions on women abiding in the self can scriptures constrain women leaving their homes?
3. When the body of a *jīvan-mukta* (spiritually liberated male) drops, whatever is done — cremation or *samādhi* (saintly burial) — so for a ripe female *yogī* leaving the body, the same is due, there is no difference.
4. A *jīvan-mukta* cannot be cremated since her body is a temple. Whatever sins follow the cremation of a liberated male, the same will accrue on the cremation of a liberated female.

(Ramaṇa Maharṣi elucidated these points regarding women's salvation on 21.8.1917 in reply to Visalakshi Ammal's question: *The Ramaṇa Gītā*: 1935: XIII.)

The debate over gender, spirituality and salvation arose in the Ramaṇāśrama in the context of the death of Ramaṇa's mother Alagammal and Ramaṇa's decision to bury rather than to cremate her. A *samādhi*[3] was built over the body of Alagammal and a temple erected on the site. Devotees now throng to this place known as Mātṛbhūteśvara temple. The temple sanctifies the worship of Pārvatī[4] in the form of a Śrī Cakra and the *devī* is offered all the traditional *ṣoḍaśopacāra* (the sixteen kinds of ritual worship) along with *kumkumārcanā* (worship with vermillion powder done for *sumaṅgalī*s[5] by *sumaṅgalī*s as well as by brāhmaṇa priests). What is interesting is that the site of such worship is the *samādhi* of a woman, especially one whom society would castigate as a widow. But Ramaṇa brushed aside all censure that followed the breaking of social norms. Not only was he unrepentent with regard to this decision on the status of a *jīvan-mukta* (irrespective of gender) but in fact personally supervised the construction of the *samādhi* temple. Regarding the last moments of Alagammal, G.V. Subbaramayya quotes Bhagavān's words: "After mother breathed her last, her body glowed with a divine resplendence. She looked not like a corpse but like a *yoginī* in meditation. . ." (Subbaramayya 1967: 41). Ramaṇa's unequivocal stand on women's right to salvation was based on his non-adherence to the conventional ways of life whether in the secular or in the spiritual path. Ramaṇa had no *guru* and was never formally initiated into *saṁnyāsa*. He preached the path of self-enquiry,

3. *Samādhi* in the present context, means the burial site of a saint although the same term is used for the trance state in meditation, and *mahāsamādhi* means the passing away of the saint in a state of trance.

4. Pārvatī is the consort of God Śiva, who is one of the divine trinity and represents the force of dissolution.

5. *Sumaṅgalī*, literally "the auspicious one," refers to a married woman, since, in the Hindu tradition, a married woman is regarded as the symbol of auspiciousness.

the practice of asking oneself "Who am I?" This path was open to man or woman, householder or renouncer, brāhmaṇa or śūdra. Ramaṇa therefore believed that self-realization which led to eternal liberation transcended sex, caste and social categories.

Ramaṇa provided the philosophical rationale behind gender attitudes within the Ramaṇāśrama in his firm conviction that the human spirit (soul?) and therefore spirituality is not conditioned by gender. It is however necessary to add that at another level Ramaṇa links himself with the entire tradition of *bhakti*, in terms of certain attitudes that cut across geographical boundaries. This is the posture of bridal mysticism which many saints, both male and female adopt, resulting in androgynous psychological behaviour and sometimes even transvestism. Subbaramayya (*Sri Ramaṇa Remniscences*: 1967) writes that Bhagavān used to narrate an incident in Mīrā Bāī's life when she met the Gosāīṅ of Mathurā. Mīrā was told that as a woman she could not enter the all-male *āśrama* of the Gosāīṅ. Mīrā retorted sharply, "I see only women around me. Lord Kṛṣṇa is the only male."

The bridal mysticism of Ramaṇa is in line with the conception that the potent creative force alone is male and all creation is female. The *Akśaramaṇi Mālāi*, literally "The garland of words"[6] has quite a few verses in which Bhagavān speaks in a female voice, as the bride of the Lord:

If after abducting me, now you do not embrace me
Where is your chivalry, Aruṇāchala!
Does it become thee to sleep
When I am being violated by others, O, Aruṇāchala!
Enfold me, body-to-body, limb-to-limb,

6. Ramaṇa Maharṣi, however, puns very cleverly on the words here, to make possible multiple layers of meanings. The poem could be interpreted as *Pearl Garland of Words* or as a *Wordy Wedding Garland*, or even as *The Immortal Garland of Ramaṇa*, if one were to split the words differently.

Or I am lost, O, Aruṇāchala!
Let us enjoy one another in the house of open space
Where there is neither night nor day, O, Aruṇāchala!

— *Akṣaramaṇi Mālāi*

tr. by G.V. Subbharamayya 1967: 64-65

At the birthday celebrations of Ramaṇa in 1939, the *Akṣaramaṇi Mālāi* was sung in Bhagavān's presence by Chanchukrishnamma, a talented lady who sang the earlier verses but shyly omitted those lines that suggested eroticism, and alternately bridal mysticism. Ramaṇa Maharṣi is said to have remarked that the chanter, as she was a woman, felt needless delicacy because she failed to understand the spiritual significance of the verses which actually transcended gender distinctions (Subbaramayya 1967: 66).

Who Were They?

Echchammal, one of the first to come, had lost husband, son and daughter by the age of 25. She was widowed, childless, destitute. She came to the *āśrama* in 1906. The spiritual bonds she formed at the *āśrama* replaced every other relationship.

Suri Nagamma came in the 1940s. She was orphaned when she was ten and widowed when she was eleven. The child, who had not even matured, began to live as an orthodox widow, serving the family and practising austerities. In her own words, "I was lying on the floor all the time and resembled a lizard clinging to the wall." In 1913 she had a yogic vision which brought her to the *āśrama*. The illiterate Suri Nagamma went on to write one of the most powerful memoirs of the Ramaṇāśrama in the 1940s and 1950s.

The story of Sampurnamma, Lokamma, Shankaramma and Brihadambal is similar.

What all these women found was serenity in the middle of suffering — an oasis of peace in a life laden with injustice.

Foreigners who gravitated to the Ramanāśram between 1900 and 1950, during Ramaṇa's lifetime, were drawn as much by the spiritual barrenness of the West as by personal sorrows. They sought love in a world besieged by hate.

While Europe was poised on the verge of Second World War, Mercedes de Acosta came to meet Ramaṇa and has left behind a powerful memoir *Here Lies the Heart.* Her inspiration — Paul Brunton. Lucy Cornelssen left war-torn Germany in 1940 to come to the *āśrama* and stay till her death in 1990. Others were missionaries and educationists like Edith Merston. Pascaline Mallet came in 1937 when Europe was divided into two armed camps and Second World War was waiting to happen. She describes "her inner spiritual ascent" climbing the red mountains Aruṇāchala in her travelogue *Turn Eastwards.*

Eleanor Pauline Noye came to the *āśrama* in 1939. Her reasons however had less to do with the war and more to do with her personal trauma. For months on end she had not slept. At the *āśrama* she says, she was filled with "ineffable peace. . . . The heartaches of yesterday and thoughts of tomorrow faded into oblivion." She began to sleep well.

Why Did They Come?

I would like to begin this section with the account of Mercedes de Acosta titled *Here Lies the Heart.* Acosta makes a couple of significant observations about the ambience of Ramaṇāśrama in around 1938:

> The *āśrama* was a small place. I remember only a stone hall where day and night Bhagavān sat on a couch. Not far from this hall, scattered around the hill, were small houses where some of the disciples lived, including his brother. . . . Once the Sage's great spiritual reputation began to spread, the *āśrama* grew larger. In my time comparatively few people journeyed to see Bhagavān and only a few Western women had ever been there.
>
> — Acosta: 1960: 290.

Lucy Cornelssen was in Germany when war broke out. The ordinary Germans faced the brunt of the war just as the average citizen anywhere in Europe. While war raged around her, a lonely and frightened Lucy lost her way and walked into a hut where she was greeted by a warm fire and a picture of Ramaṇa Maharṣi.

Guided by destiny, she found her way to the Ramaṇāśrama where she lived till her death in 1990 at the age of 93. She was known as Satyamayi (the name she took) or as Lucy Ma. Her autobiography *Hunting the "I"* is a self-reflexive exploration of her spiritual journey.

Ethel Gladys Merston served tirelessly the wounded soldiers in Belgium during the First World War. She was awarded an OBE by the British queen in 1918. When the freedom struggle commenced in India, Merston became a follower of Gandhi. She adopted a village in northern India where she ran a free dispensary. In 1944 she drifted into the Ramaṇāśrama and stayed on for years.

The most recurrent pattern in the lives of the Indian women who came to seek refuge at Ramaṇāśrama is destitution, widowhood and great personal suffering. Ramaṇa's presence provided the healing touch, restored their sense of dignity and purpose in life and turned them gently on to the path of spirituality. The metamorphosis of these women into spiritual aspirants occurred slowly but surely at the Ramaṇāśrama. The instances of women coming to Ramaṇāśrama on a spiritual quest initially were rare though not wholly unknown.

Echchammal (Mandakolathur Lakshmiammal) was a sad woman. Before she turned twenty-five she had lost husband, son and daughter in quick succession. In the prime of her life she was left widowed, childless, destitute. There was nothing but pain and darkness in her life. Narasimhaswami, recounting her life says that she could not bear even to open her window, for if she did she would at once look upon the school where her daughter (who had died prematurely) had passed several happy years of study. Echchammal began to go on pilgrimages to assuage her grief. She met many sages but none could help her. When she returned to her village in 1906 she was told about the silent young Yogi on Mount Aruṇāchala.

Echchammal came to the Ramaṇāśrama in 1906. She stayed in the town since women were not allowed within the *āśrama* after 6:00 p.m. On beholding Bhagavān the next day she felt the bundle of sorrow drop down. The memory of her husband and children no longer caused pain and bitterness. Later she adopted a girl Chellammal who died some time after giving birth to a boy named Ramaṇa. In the words of Lord Kṛṣṇa quoted by Narasimha Swami:

> *yasyānugraham icchāmi tasya sarvam haramyaham*
>
> Whenever I wish to bless anyone, everything he calls his/hers, I snatch away. — Narasimha Swami 1993: 102

The spiritual bond she formed with the Maharṣi now replaced every relationship Echchammal had shared as wife or mother. In 1907 she started serving food to Bhagavān in the Virūpākśa cave and thenceforth dedicated her life to service at the Ramaṇāśrama.

Suri Nagamma was a child widow. She had been orphaned when she was ten and widowed when she was eleven. The child who had not even matured, was forced to lead the life of an orthodox Hindu widow — serving the family, practising austerities and reading sacred books. She felt her very presence to be sinful and shunned human contact. In her own words: "I was lying on the floor all the time on a torn mat, my hand for a pillow and resembled a lizard clinging to the wall" (Nagamma 1975: 1). She was illiterate and hence the last outlet was also denied to her. It was in 1913 that she had the vision of a sage in yogic posture unto whom she was to surrender everything almost thirty years later.

In 1918 she learnt to read and write Telugu at Bezawada from a literary-minded lady Indumati. Nagamma used her newly acquired skill to pour forth her heart in 108 verses in a composition called *Manasa Shatakam,* being essentially catechisms addressed to her own mind. When Nagamma moved to Vijayawāḍā in order to pursue a life of meditation and reading, the women of the orthodox brāhmaṇa community rebuked her saying that she was unfit for a spiritual life or for initiation into any *mantra* as she had not shaven her hair like all orthodox widows. Somehow Nagamma never shaved her head as she had the shining example of Tarikoṇḍa Veṅkaṭamba, a great saint who was also a child-widow. When Veṅkaṭamba's relatives forcibly tried to shave her head, blood gushed out forcing them to stop (another version is that when the newly shaven Veṅkaṭamba emerged after a dip in the river her hair had grown down to her waist!). Tarikoṇḍa Veṅkaṭamba was the celebrated composer of *Veṅkaṭacala Māhatmyam, Rājayoga Sāraṁ,* etc. To help Nagamma get over her intense depression it was suggested that she should stay in Tiruvannamalai with Devulapalli Subbamma (Subbalakshmiammal) who was serving in the *āśrama* kitchen. It was thus that in July 1941 Suri Nagamma reached Ramaṇāśrama after offering prayers at Kalahasti and Tirupati. Suri Nagamma writes that the concentrated gaze from Ramaṇa's luminous eyes washed away all the ignorance of her mind. She considers this itself as his initiation. Spontaneously Nagamma composed eight verses called *Śaraṇāgati* (literally "surrender") signifying her "surrender" at the feet of Ramaṇa Maharṣi.

Suri Nagamma's relative Subbalakshmiammal who had preceded her to Ramaṇāśrama had a similar background of widowhood and destitution. Widowed at the age of sixteen she says that she was sent back to her mother's house in Nellore to live as a widow should live. After going on pilgrimages Subbalakshmiammal was planning to settle down in Varanasi with her friend Parvatamma. However, Subbalakshmiammal's destiny took her to the Ramaṇāśrama, to be an assistant in the kitchen. Ramaṇa also entrusted her with tasks like making multiple handwritten copies of *Aruṇācala Śatakam.*

Sampurnamma's life replicates that of Subbalakshmiammal so closely that an account of it would be tedious were it not so painful. A childless widow, her life followed the endless rigmarole of desolation and despair. The turning point in her life came while she was worshipping in Madurai. An old brāhmaṇa asked her, "Won't you cook a meal for me"? When she offered to take him to her home after worship, she found on her return from the temple that he had vanished. In 1932, when she saw Ramaṇa, she connected him with her vision. She took charge of the kitchen and was assisted by Ramaṇa himself. She says:

> The kitchen was small at that time and every time I needed to move I would go around him and take good care to have him on my right hand. Thus I would perform numerous *pradakṣiṇāms* during the day. Was he not my God? Was I not fortunate to have him in the very middle of my kitchen?
>
> — *Ramaṇa Smṛti,* tr. G. Venkatachalam: 1980

The story of Lokamma, Shankaramma, and Brihadambal is essentially the same as the ones recounted above and vary only in the specificities of time and place. Brihadambal of Ramanathapuram summed it up neatly when she said "Only *amaṅgalīs* (widows) come here, not *sumaṅgalīs*" (Interview dated 24.3.1994).

Almost true but not entirely so. For "Jatini" Sundarambal it was from the beginning a spiritual quest. She was the daughter of a lawyer at Tiruvallur near Madras (Chennai). When she went to her husband's place after marriage she developed a bad headache. No treatment was of any use. She returned to her parents' place and her headache disappeared. This phenomenon repeated itself so often that her husband took pity on her and allowed her to return to her parental home.

She visited the Ramaṇāśrama for the first time with her father and accompanied Bhagavān on his *Giri Pradakṣiṇam* (circumambulating the hill). She returned again to Tiruvannamalai after a few months and stayed with Echchammal. She came for Bhagavān's *darśan* on the first day but did not come on the second day. Echchammal informed Ramaṇa that Sundarambal was on a fast for twenty-one days. She usually took a vow of silence and always bathed in cold water. Since she never combed her hair it became "matted" and she came to be known as "Jatini" (one whose locks are matted). Sundarambal left the *āśrama* without disclosing her destination and hence the rest of her spiritual career is unchartered.

Another woman named Sundarammal came to the Ramaṇāśrama in a most curious manner in 1933. Widowed very young she was confined to the four walls of her wealthy home. In 1932 she happened to hear an account of Ramaṇa's extraordinary life by an āśramite at the nearby temple in Madras. From then on she had an intense desire to go to Tiruvannamalai, which her father refused to fulfil. On the first of January, 1933, she had a strange vision. At 3 o'clock in the early hours of the morning she received a sudden blow on her side. The Maharṣi had materialized near her beside her pillow. "Now is the time; come," he said. She followed him downstairs at which point the Maharṣi vanished. After a few minutes a rickshaw stopped in front of her home and the rikshaw-puller asked, "Are you Sundarammal?" An old *sādhu* came and woke me up and told me to put you in a bus. With great hesitation she who had never stepped out of her sheltered home went with this unknown man. Since there was no direct bus to Tiruvannamalai she got into one going up to Ginji or Tindivanam. On the way her bus passed another one that was coming from the opposite direction. Someone got down from it and climbed up into her bus asking if there was a certain Sundarammal there? "Yes, here I am," she told him. He told her that Bhagavān (Ramaṇa) had sent him to find her. Since she had no money Sundarammal sold her gold earrings and reached Tiruvannamalai at dusk. Since in the thirties women could not enter the precincts of the *āśrama* after sunset Sundarammal could meet Ramaṇa only the next day. On seeing her, he said "Ah, so you have come at last"! Sundarammal embraced the feet of Bhagavān fervently and chanted the famous Sanskrit verse:

tvam eva mātā ca pitā tvameva . . .
You are my mother, my father, my brother,
You are my whole family, all my wealth,
You are my all, absolutely all, O my lord!

Her parents sent her brothers to bring her back by force, if necessary. Sundarammal threatened suicide and told them, "They are only the father and mother of this body. Here I have discovered the father of my spirit. I shall never leave."

During the last fifteen years of the Maharṣi's life, she never once left Tiruvannamalai. This account of her entry into Ramaṇāśrama was told by Sundarammal herself to Swami Abhishiktananda and recounted by him in his book, *The Secret of Arunachala* (Delhi: 1979).

Many other women, destitutes, widows and in some rare cases as with Ḳanakamma, spiritually oriented women drifted into the Ramaṇāśrama between 1920 and 1940. Gauri Ammal came to Bhagavān with her father even before her marriage but came to stay permanently after she was widowed. Her only daughter Saroja wears ochre and is a permanent resident of Tiruvannamalai. Shantamma, Subbalakshmiammal, Sampurnamma and Alamelu Ammal drifted towards the *āśrama* between these two decades. Alamelu (called Amulu) was closely related to Gauri Ammal and is my Grand Aunt. A child widow, she was self-taught and could speak six languages fluently. Besides serving in the kitchen she sometimes acted as interpreter in the *āśrama*.

Tesur Akhilandamma, in terms of her life pattern — widowhood at the age of seven, loneliness and destitution — ought logically to fall into the earlier category of devotees like Echchammal and Suri Nagammal but in terms of her spiritual situation she comes closer to the latter category. Her's appears to be one of the few autobiographical accounts left behind by women. This was published in 1961 under the title *Ramaṇānubhavam*. Unlike Suri Nagamma, there is no trace of any personal bereavement in her writings, only renunciation and spiritual surrender. Tesuramma was not a scholar but a nurturing mother figure for Ramaṇa. Along with Echchammal, Mudaliyar Patti and her daughter-in-law Kamākṣī, she began the practice of serving food to Ramaṇa and continued with it even after Alagammal had provided Ramaṇāśrama with its own kitchen. It is said that Tesuramma found an ochre robe (signifying the robe of the ascetic) in one of the tiffin carriers in which she carried food to Bhagavān. She regarded this event as her miraculous initiation into *saṁnyāsa,* the ascetic path.

Janaki Mātā stands in a peculiar position in relation to the Bhagavān *vis-à-vis* her social situation. She was not a widow, nor was she celibate. She came to Ramaṇa even while her husband was alive. At the age of fourteen she married a thirty-two year old doctor of her own choice. She moved in high social circles and was president of several ladies clubs, charity clubs, etc. During her visit to the *āśrama,* Bhagavān gave her a copy of the *Upadeśa Sāram* in Malayalam and this she regarded as her initiation. She frequently went into a trance and was reputed to possess miraculous powers. She seems to have worn saffron (even during her husband's lifetime) and closely associated herself with Ramaṇa. A brief write-up on her appears in the 1966 issue of *The Mountain Path.* When she was told by others that Bhagavān never initiated anyone, she wept before Bhagavān, who told her: "Who told you that you have no *guru*? I am here as your *guru*. Nothing will upset your mind." Janaki Mātā, however, was never an āśramite. Kanakamma, an old devotee of Ramaṇa, told me that Janaki Mātā had her own followers who called her "Guru Ma." She seems to have gravitated towards Ramaṇa following an unusual occurrence in her spiritual career. On 12 October 1937, at mid-night she felt a powerful explosion in the back of her head. She went to Bhagavān in order to get his blessings for channelling this surging spiritual force which had come from the bursting of the *kuṇḍalinī śakti* (Janaki Mātā's experience as reported in the *Mountain Path*, January 1966).

The last of these women is also the most important, the one who is the presiding force of the Matṛbhūteśvara temple, Ramaṇa's mother Alagammal. The first time she came it was to plead with her son to come back home. She came to Pavazhakkunru in 1898, saw the matted hair and emaciated body of her son and begged him to come with her. His response was to write on a piece of paper:

> The ordainer controls the fate of souls in accordance with their past deeds — their *prārabdha karma*. Whatever is destined not to happen will not happen, try how hard you may. Whatever is destined to happen will happen, do what you may to stop it. This is certain. The best course, therefore, is for one to remain silent.
>
> — Tr. from Tamil by Narasimhaswami, rpt. 1993: 66

Alagammal failed to win back her son but herself returned to Tiruvannamalai in 1916, this time as a spiritual aspirant and āśramite. She soon became a mother figure for all at the *āśrama*. Ramaṇa's mother, Alagammal, was initially motivated to settle down at the Ramaṇāśrama neither by personal suffering nor by spiritual intensity but by her motherliness and practical exigencies. Having limited economic resources and no other refuge, she finally came to settle down at the Ramaṇāśrama. Her life underwent a gradual but radical transformation from mother to disciple, from one who exercised loving authority over her son Ramaṇa to one who made a spiritual surrender at the feet of Guru Ramaṇa. This transformation then makes Alagammal the foremost of Ramaṇa's women devotees. She attained *samādhi* in 1922.

This section would be complete only with the narration of how Ramaṇa himself called Lucy Cornelssen to the Ramaṇāśrama in Tiruvannamalai. Although "Lucy Ma," as she came to be known later, did not encounter Ramaṇa Maharṣi in the flesh, she was magnetically drawn to Ramaṇāśrama following an encounter with his astral body in the year 1939 (or 1940). While she was groping about helplessly one night in the war-torn Germany, having lost the way to her house, she found that the door of a hut was ajar. When she walked in she saw on the table a photograph of a man with the most extraordinarily luminous eyes. This, she was told, was Ramaṇa, the sage of Tiruvannamalai. It was in answer to His spiritual call that Lucy Ma came to Ramaṇāśrama and stayed on till 1990, passing away at the ripe old age of 92. She lived and worked in the Ramaṇāśrama for nearly forty years.

What Did They Do? Āśramite Life

It was the early women devotees of Ramaṇa who performed the role of nurturing mothers to the Maharṣi and his select disciples. Keerai Patti (literally the "spinach grandmother") was an old woman who supplied Ramaṇa and his devotees with rice gruel and spinach, even at the turn of the century before the *āśrama* had come into being. Tesur Akhilandammaiyar and Echchammal followed suit. There were many other women, lost to our collective memory, who served and nurtured the young brāhmaṇa Swami and his band of devotees in the pre-āśramite days. The Skandāśrama came to be used as a hermitage by Ramaṇa around the 1930s. It was perhaps in keeping with the Hindu ethos that the women, who came from near and far to the shelter of Ramaṇāśrama, gravitated towards the kitchen. In those days, i.e. the early decades of the twentieth century, women were not allowed to stay beyond dusk in the *āśrama*. *Āśrama* rules, none of which were of Ramaṇa's making, kept women on the periphery of *āśrama* life merely on account of their sex. Women like Echchamal and Keerapatti stood outside the *āśrama* fraternity. Things however changed somewhat with the coming of Alagammal. She had come once to Tiruvannamalai in 1898 in order to persuade her ascetic son to return home but by 1916 she had returned to stay permanently in the shelter of her son. It was she who started the *āśrama* kitchen, thus providing the necessary initial space for women, destitutes and devotees. Her role as the nurturing mother now extended to all the āśramites. The kitchen had in a sense become the heart of the *āśrama* and women were in a dominant position within its sacred space.

Among the earliest women to serve in the kitchen were Shantammal in 1927 and Sampurnammal in 1930. Shantammal had been cooking all her life — first for her husband and after he died, for her three sons. She lost all her sons and went to serve her daughter and son-in-law. At her daughter's death, she found herself keeping house for the brother of her brother's wife. At forty years of age, Shantammal had seen nothing outside the kitchen of various homes. But at forty she wondered where her life would end — was kitchen work her life's only goal? As she commenced her spiritual quest, one Nagasami initiated her into the *mahāmantra*. With this the pilgrim's progress had begun. Shantammal spent the next nine years reading holy books and expounding them to housewives and widows in her native town of Ramnad. At the age of fifty, she met Ramaṇa and took over the charge of the kitchen from the Maharṣi's brother, Chinnasvami. As with brother Lawrence, kitchen work in the Ramaṇāśrama paved the way to salvation for Subbalakshmiammal, whose hunch backed figure became familiar to visitors:

> I was put in charge of the cooking and Bhagavān would come often to help. Could I dream of greater happiness. . . . With him near me I was tireless. I worked with God. Whoever has not experienced the ecstasy of grinding, the rapture of cooking, the joy of serving iddlies to devotees, the state when the mind is in the heart and the heart is in Him and He is in the work, cannot know how much bliss the human heart contains. — *Ramaṇa Smṛti*: 1980

Bhagavān in his turn provided Subbalakshmiammal with spiritual sustenance. He gave her copies of his *Upadeśa Sāram* and *Ulladu Narpatu* (*The Forty Catechisms*) and initiated her into self-enquiry. Shantammal testifies to spiritual experiences, like seeing a light in the point between the eyebrows, and her whole being becoming flooded with light. Sampurnammal also attests to having had similar spiritual experiences and tells her interviewer that Bhagavān asked her to read *Who Am I* and the *Ribhu Gita* even though she pleaded stupidity in Vedāntic matters (Conversation with G.Venkatachalam, *Montain Path*, 1980: no page numbers).

Shantammal in her account also describes the arrival of a new spiritual entrant at the *āśrama* — the cow Lakṣmī. Lakṣmī was gifted to the *āśrama* as the result of a villager's inner voice that urged him that she rightfully belonged to the Ramaṇāśrama. The cow Lakṣmī was widely believed by the devotees (the Maharṣi himself remained silent on the subject) to be an incarnation of Keerai Patti and the Maharṣi is often said to have remarked that they both belonged to Guḍiyaṭṭam. Like other devotees she sat in meditation in the hall, and once the Maharṣi remarked to Shantammal that Lakṣmī was in deep *samādhi*.

Her niece Brihadambal, who at the ripe old age of 85 still lives in Ramaṇāśrama, followed Shantammal of Ramaṇathapuram. Among the other women who played the role of cooks and servers in the Ramaṇāśrama were: Tenammal of Tirumangalam, Lakṣmī Ammal of Tiruchchuzhi (the Maharṣi's native place), Lokammal of Pattadakkurichchi, Sampurnammal of Vathrayiruppu (she came around the same time as Shantammal), Subbalakshmiammal and Shankarammal. What is striking about this long list of the early women in the *āśrama* is that they were, without exception, widows. Interestingly these women, quite a few of whom were destitutes, perceived their work in the kitchen as the gateway to freedom and salvation. It was very different from the drudgery a widow within a patriarchal home is subjected to. These women had stepped out of their thresholds, become a part of monastic living and spent their time in doing the only thing they knew — cooking in the common kitchen. In contradistinction to the patriarchal home where it would be inauspicious for a widow to be seen anywhere other than the kitchen or the worship room, the widows at the Ramaṇāśrama sat in the meditation hall with the men, the literate among them read and even translated philosophical works and engaged in lengthy debates with the Maharṣi.

The widow having her menstrual periods within an orthodox Brāhmanical home would have been segregated as doubly impure, but Sampurnamma comes out with a striking counter story in the Ramaṇāśrama. Usually during her menstrual periods, she would arrange for someone to feed her but once there was no one to bring her even gruel. Starved and miserable, she was sitting in some abandoned stone structure away from the *āśrama*. Ramaṇa asked for her and was told about her segregation. He ordered, "Ask her to come and sit with us. Feed her in a decent manner." When they protested saying she was impure, the Maharṣi thundered: "Who here is pure and who is impure?" (Sampurnammal conversation with G. Venkatachalam: *Ramaṇa Smṛti* 1980). This incident strengthens one's conviction that despite kitchen work being a common factor in the lives of widows and āśramites, the crucial difference lay in the widow being incarcerated within kitchen walls, while the *āśrama* kitchen was the gateway to self-respect and self-expression for women.

The plucking of flowers for daily worship and the fashioning of garlands was another major activity performed entirely by women in the *āśrama*. Among the garland makers during Ramaṇa's lifetime, Pushpammal of Thellar is still remembered for her pious disposition.

Women also acted as copiers for the Ramaṇāśrama. Subbalakshmiammal, who served in the kitchen, was often assigned the task of making multiple copies of Ramaṇa's writings, which were not intended for printing but for private circulation in the initial stage. She has narrated the incident of Bhagavān asking her to copy *Aruṇācala Aṣṭakam*. Both Uma Devi and Pankajakshiammal, and her mother Uma Deviyar, have been ardent devotees of Ramaṇa. Uma Devi perceived Ramaṇa as her child and composed "cradle songs" called *tālāttu* on him. It is said that when she was blessed with the vision of the Maharṣi as her divine child, she lactated even though she was past the age of child-bearing! (Interview with Pankajakshiammal on 23.2.1995 at Tiruvannamalai). Uma Devi's daughter, Pankajakshiammal, who is still living at the Ramaṇāśrama, has also composed many songs on Ramaṇa and his philosophy. Perhaps Pankajakshiammal's most useful contribution to the *āśrama* life has been to put together the biographies of the āśramites, especially the women. In this task she has been collaborating with the renowned Ramaṇa devotee, Kunjusvamigal, who passed away in 1993. Another composer of poetic verses in the Ramaṇāśrama was Lakshmiammal (Lakṣmī Ranganadham). However, the *āśrama* authorities have no record whatsoever of her prolific writings.

She wrote a poetic biography of Bhagavān Ramaṇa called *Ramaṇa Vijayam* and another composition in verse called *Ramaṇa Mānasam* of 108 verses, exhorting the mind to hold on firmly to the lotus feet of Maharṣi if salvation was the goal of life.

Meenakshiammal, the wife of Sri Muruganar, maintained a private diary recording her experiences at Ramaṇāśrama. This handwritten manuscript is in the Ramaṇa archives but unpublished. The text is a perfect example of what Western feminists like Alain Showalter would call "quilting" in terms of its homely, even quotidian expressions and concerns. Nevertheless its contents, which most of the present administrators of the *āśrama* have tended to dismiss as "trivia", reflects the life and reactions of the women āśramites and is a powerful document in many ways.

By far the most important of the women āśramites was Suri Nagammal. A child widow, who was married when she was eleven, and widowed by the time she was twelve, she had been forced into a widow's weeds even before she could experience marriage. She suffered all the tortures of loneliness and social ostracism till the age of forty, around which time she arrived at the Ramaṇāśrama due largely to her vision of Ramaṇa. Nagamma began to spend all her days in the presence of Maharṣi and was hence witness to the theological debates that went on around Ramaṇa, the arrival and departure of Indian and foreign devotees, spiritual experiences of the āśramites and the problems of administering a rapidly growing monastic institution.

The products of Suri Nagamma's observations of and at the Ramaṇāśrama are the now famous *Letters from the Ramaṇāśrama,* which she wrote to her brother T.S. Shastri between November 1945 and 1948. In all, three hundred letters were written which constitute the most authentic documents of Ramaṇāśrama of those years. It is noteworthy that in 1947 the *āśrama* administrator and the Maharṣi's younger brother forbade Nagamma to write these letters and after the initial publication of 75 letters in July 1947, confiscated all the rest. She was made to promise that she would not write anymore. The personal diary of another devotee Venkataramayya had been similarly confiscated (Nagamma 1974: 30-33; 46-47). Nagamma writes that the Maharṣi himself expressed surprise at this enforced silence and subtly encouraged her to transgress the unreasonable *āśrama* rules since it was in a good cause (Nagamma 1974: 51-53). At present the *āśrama* authorities have been taking much pains to print the letters written by Suri Nagamma published by the Ramaṇa Trust as *Letters from the Ramaṇāśrama* by Suri Nagamma, Tiruvannamalai, South India, 1970.

In her early years at the Ramaṇāśrama, between 1943 and 1945, Suri Nagamma produced many poems. Her first poem was aptly titled *Śaraṇāgati* meaning "Surrender." She wrote:

> *I saw Him and He saw me*
> *The lustre was so strong*
> *that my head bowed down with shyness.*

This poem was followed by one titled *Āśrama and the Maharṣi* and then *Prārthanā* which means "Prayer." Then followed almost a flood of verses called: *Daivapatham* (a long poem of twenty-seven stanzas on the splendour of Maharṣi's eyes), *Nakṣatramālā* (star studded garland), and *Arpaṇa* (offering). These poems along with *Prārthanā* and *Śaraṇāgati*, all of which were written in Telugu, were compiled together by one Srinivasa Mauni under the title *Ramaṇa Karuṇā Vilāsam*. One of her earliest compositions written, in the 1920s, was the *Mānasa Śatakam*, a book of hundred and eight verses, which was on her spiritual struggle and the quest for a *sadguru*. Her work *Bālakṛṣṇa Gītāvalī* also contained a hundred and eight verses in which she experimented with the technique of *Ātmopāsanā*, that is worship of the Self by the self. The Self itself was Balakrishna and her mind was the lovelorn Gopikā.

The later years of Nagamma's life were spent away from the Ramaṇāśrama in Vijayawada and it was at this time in the 1970s that she wrote her autobiography, which was translated into English by her brother D.S. Shastri and published as *My Life at Śrī Ramaṇāśrama* (Sri Ramaṇāśrama Trust, Tiruvannamalai, 1975). It is important to note here that Suri Nagamma's entire literary output was in Telugu.

This book is in many ways a remarkable historical document. Ever since her widowhood at the age of twelve there was great social pressure on her family to shave her head, but Suri Nagamma refused to accede to this barbarous custom. In her autobiography she says that she was inspired by the example of a distant relative, called Kaivarupu Balamba, who on her widowhood had refused to remove her hair. Balamba had opted for living away from the family and sustaining herself by running a feeding house. Suri Nagamma thus successfully defied patriarchal social norms by retaining her long hair. Her reminiscences at the Ramaṇāśrama include many similar narratives that would interest the feminist scholars of today.

T.R. Kanakamma was present in the *āśrama* during the last decade of Ramaṇa's life. What predominates in Kanakamma's many writings is not so much the devotional element as her Advaita (Vedāntic monism) philosophy and great dispassion or *vairāgya*. She has authored the commentary on Ramaṇa's texts, which has been published as *Upadesa Noonmālai* (Ramaṇāśrama, Tiruvannamalai, 1991). Recently in 1991, Kanakammal published a short biography of Sri Muruganar titled *Sri Muruganar* [in Tamil], the devotee responsible for codifying the *āśrama* prayer rituals into the *Sannidhi Murai*, which became a catechism of worship for the *āśrama*.

Apart from their participation in *āśrama* life as cooks, servers, garland makers, poets and diarists, women have also played a keyrole in maintaining the Ramaṇāśrama library. Suri

Nagamma worked at the circulation counter in the library and was specifically put in charge of all books concerning Telugu literature. During the later years of the Ramaṇāśrama, when thousands began to throng the place for the Maharṣi's *darśan*, Suri Nagamma was also put in charge of regulating the crowds of women devotees. Alameluamma, my grand aunt, was also a child widow who was a practising Gandhian and did her daily quota of hand spinning. She not only translated Gandhi's works into Tamil but also acted as interpreter at the *āśrama* since she was proficient in as many as fourteen languages. She was entirely self-taught because widows were not permitted to attend school.

Any account of the contribution of women to the Ramaṇāśrama would be incomplete without a reference to Lucy Cornelssen known at Tiruvannamalai as "Lucy Ma." She lived by herself in a small wayside shrine on the *Giri Pradakṣiṇa* road (the path one took going around the sacred mountain) and practised meditation. Under the nom-de-plume of Satyamayi she translated the Maharṣi's works like *Who Am I* and *The Forty Catechisms* into German. Perhaps Lucy Ma's greatest intellectual contribution is her book *Hunting the I* (Sri Ramaṇāśrama, Tiruvannamalai, 1979). This is perhaps the most brilliant as well as the most lucid of the innumerable commentaries on Ramaṇa's philosophy of self-enquiry. Lucy Cornelssen also wrote her autobiography in German, which would have been an invaluable document of women's perceptions of the Ramaṇāśrama, but unfortunately this document is not accessible, let alone in an English translation. The same problem of non-availability haunts the diaries left behind by two other women, both of whom had interacted closely with Ramaṇa. One was Lucy Osborne whose diary was to have been edited jointly by her husband and herself as *Our Quest*. One chapter of it was published in the *Mountain Path*, 1970. The book was never completed and Lucy's daughter Kitty Osborne, who lives in Tiruvannamalai, in the vicinity of the Ramaṇāśrama, told me that Lucy's diary might be too private for general viewing (conversation with Kitty Osborne, 14 January. 1995). The other devotee, Ethel Merston, died without publishing her diary, which she had concealed for long from the *āśrama* authorities.

Of War and Peace: Concluding Thoughts

The quest for a spiritual life is the binding force among the inmates of Ramaṇāśrama, men and women. Whether employed in the kitchen, the library or as copiers and translators, the journey inwards into the self has been a constant factor with them. Perhaps this should be noted especially in the case of women since grinding, pounding and cooking, which they did for the major part of their time, do not appear to be spiritual practices. Subbalakshmiammal clarifies this point in her reporting of a conversation with the Maharṣi. She writes that, despite being at the Ramaṇāśrama, she was still frustrated and wanted to go to Varanasi for pursuing a spiritual path. She then narrates the following incident:

> One day Bhagavān was looking at me intently and said, "It looks as if you are still hankering after meditation."
>
> I replied, "What have I got except endless work in the kitchen"?
>
> Bhagavān said: "Your hands may do the work but your mind can remain still. You are that which never moves. Realize that and you will find work is not a strain. But as long as you think that you are the body and that the work is done by you, you will feel your life to be an endless toil. In fact it is the mind which toils, not the body. Even if your body keeps quiet will your mind keep quiet too?"
>
> — *Ramaṇa Smṛti*: tr. G.Venkatachalam 1980

"Jatini" Sundarambal (literally "Sundarambal with the matted hair"), acquired her nickname "Jatini" because her hair had become matted as a result of her austerities. After being in the Ramaṇāśrama for a number of years, she went on a pilgrimage to the Himalayas, after which the *āśrama* lost track of her. It is recorded by Kunjuswami, in his diary published as *Reminiscences*, that "Jatini" Sundarambal posed a number of philosophical questions to the Maharṣi which he clarified. Unfortunately, Kunjuswami has recorded neither her questions nor his answers that could have served as useful pointers to the direction of her spiritual quest. Kunjuswami, however, does say that the Maharṣi recollected the story of Choodala and Shikhidhvaja, in response to Sundarambal's queries (Kunjuswami 1992: 95-97). According to this story, contained in the scripture *Yoga Vāsiṣṭha,* Queen Choodala was a self-realized soul who initiated her husband into the spiritual path. Shikhidhvaja, her husband, wrongly associated spirituality with renunciation. Choodala, his wife and *guru,* instructed him that being constantly centred on the Self, one could perform any task including governance of the country, without being tainted by it. The Maharṣi mentioned this story not only to "Jatini" Sundarambal but also to Subbalakshmiammal. The extraordinary value of the story of Choodala lies not only in her exemplifying Ramaṇa's philosophical dictum "inactivity in activity," but also in her being the prime example of gender role reversal by becoming the *guru* of her own husband. It is noteworthy that the woman saint, Avudaiammal, has written a long poem on Choodala in Tamil entitled "Choodala Kummi," published in the journal *Shankara Kripa,* Tiruchchirapalli (July 1964 to June 1965) by Gomati Rajangam. Feminists could analyse this as an excellent example of women's subjectivity in the spiritual realm, since the story of queen Choodala is turned into a dance-song (*kummi* being a powerful mode of audio-visual expression by women in Tamil culture) by an eighteenth-century woman saint, Avudaiammal, and picked up for editing and publishing with a special commentary by another woman renunciate, Gomati Rajangam (aunt of the celebrated Tamil poet Subramanya Bharatiyar).

It is by and large through the writings of the foreign women devotees that one gets an idea of the kind of questions that these women posed to the Maharṣi and the philosophical and spiritual responses he provided. Foreign women, with the exception of a few like Lucy Osborne, Ethel Merston and above all Lucy Cornelssen, did not stay for any length of time at the Ramaṇāśrama. Any questions posed to the Maharṣi usually boomeranged on the visitor in the form of the Maharṣi's response: "Find out who it is that questions". But surprisingly, when Mercedes de Acosta asked the Maharṣi in desperation:

> "Tell me–whom shall I follow — what shall I follow"? . . . "What about religious teachers, *gurus*"?

The Maharṣi replied:

> You should follow the self. There is nothing and no one else to follow. . . . Can religion, which teaches you to look outside yourself, which promises a heaven and a reward outside yourself, can this help you? It is only by diving deep into the spiritual heart that one can find the self.

Mercedes de Acosta writes, "He placed his right hand on my right breast and continued"

> Here lies the Heart, the Dynamic, Spiritual Heart. It is called Hridaya and is located on the right side of the chest and is clearly visible to the inner eye of an adept on the spiritual path. Through meditation you can learn to find the self in the cave of this heart. — Mercedes de Costa: 1960: 292

The spiritual path of the inmates of the Ramaṇāśrama lay in silent self-enquiry. Meditation and renunciation were mental postures and had nothing to do with the ochre robe and austerities.

The definitive conclusion that emerges from the lives and accounts of the women, who lived at the Ramaṇāśrama in the Maharṣi's lifetime, is that for them the path of "hunting the I" lay through the vistas of silence and self-reflection. Their reward lay in the annihilation of the self, end of all duality, all hatred and the feeling of infinite peace and tranquillity.

I would like to conclude with a story, which is not about a woman but a man. In 1916, the third year of the great war, a young man was waiting on a platform, in a little Polish village, waiting for the train which would take him to the frontline and maybe to his death. In the autumn night, a falling star caught his eye and he wished for "Love" of all things. "Love" to him was the antidote to a war that was not of his making, Love alone could take him, from the world of dark terror he was entering, to a world bathed in peace and tranquillity. Thirty years later he found true love in Ramaṇa and his *āśrama*. The man was Sudoski, who lost his name and identity and became Mauni Sadhu, the author of *In days of Great Peace.*

The Universal Self counters the divisive selves
love replaces hate
and fear and terror
give way to tranquility in the Ramaṇāśrama.

References

Abhishiktananda, 1979, *The Secret of Aruṇāchala*. New Delhi: ISCPK.

Acosta, Mercedes de., 1960, *Here Lies the Heart*. New York: Reynal and Co.

Akhilandammal, Tesur., 1961, *Ramaṇanubhavam* (in Tamil). Tamil Nadu: Tesur.

Cornelssen, Lucy, 1979, *Hunting the I*. Tiruvannamalai: Ramaṇāśrama.

Ganapati Muni Kavya Kanta, 1992 (Ist edn. 1935), *Ramaṇa Gītā,* Sanskrit text with English tr. by Viswanatha Swami and K. Swamiratha, Sri Ramaṇāśrama, Tiruvannamalai.

Ganesan, V, 1990, *Moments Remembered: Remininiscences of Bhagavān Ramaṇa.* Tiruvannamalai: Ramaṇāśrama.

Janaki Mātā Sri, 1966, *Shashtyabhdapoorty Souvenir*. Tanjavur: Celebrations Committee Publication.

Kanakammal, T.R., 1991, *Sri Muruganar* (in Tamil). Tiruvannamalai: Ramaṇāśrama.

Kanakammal, T.R., 1991, *Upadesa Noonmalai* (in Tamil with commentary). Tiruvannamalai: Ramaṇāśrama.

Kunjuswami, 1980, *"Enadu ninaivugal"* (in Tamil) tr. into English as *Reminiscences* by K. Subrahmanian. Tiruvannamalai: Sri Ramaṇāśrama.

Mallet, Pascaline, 1937, *Turn Eastwards: Glimpses into Indian Life*. London: Rider and Co.

Mountain Path Journal, quarterly (1964 January onwards). Tiruvannamalai: Ramaṇāśrama.

Mudaliyar, Devarja A., n/d., *The Cow Lakṣmī*. Tiruvannamalai: Sri Ramaṇāśrama.

Nagamma, Suri, 1975, *My Life at Sri Ramaṇāśrama*. Tiruvannamalai: Ramaṇāśrama.

Nagamma, Suri, 1970, *Letters from Sri Ramaṇāśrama*. Tiruvannamalai: Ramaṇāśrama.

Narasimhaswami, B.V., 1993, *Self-Realisation: Life and Teachings of Ramaṇa Maharṣi*. Tiruvannamalai: Ramaṇāśrama.

Ramaṇa Smṛti, 1980, Tiruvannamalai: Ramaṇāśrama.

Swaminathan, K., 1975, *Ramaṇa Maharṣi.* New Delhi: National Book Trust.

Subbaramayya, G.V., 1967, *Sri Ramaṇa Reminiscences*. Tiruvannamalai: Sri Ramaṇāśrama.

PANELS

Panel No. 1
Journey into Openness

10

Understandings of Interreligious Dialogue

Mary N. MacDonald

As members of the Education Committee of the InterReligious Council of Central New York, our concern is to educate the Central New York community about the diverse religious traditions in our community and to foster collaboration in the projects supported by the InterReligious Council . Our mission statement says that dialogue is one of the ways that the Education Committee of the InterReligious Council (IRC) goes about its work. Each of us brings a particular background to this work. In my case I have been an elementary school teacher in Australia, a missionary teacher working with adults in Papua New Guinea, and, for the past eighteen years a college teacher in Central New York. As a missionary and as a teacher I have had many opportunities to think about dialogue. I have thought of it in relation to communication across cultures; I have regarded it as a teaching and learning technique; I have experienced it as conversation within and between religions. This afternoon I shall talk about kinds of dialogue, goals of dialogue, and problems of dialogue, particularly as they apply to the work of the IRC, but also as they affect all of us who live in a religiously plural world. Since 11 September 2001, it has become imperative that we foster wholistic dialogues that engage us with the hopes and the sufferings of the communities in our midst and communities around the world. Those of us on the panel this afternoon welcome the opportunity to make more explicit the principles which implicitly guide our work. The congress is an occasion for us to revise and refine our own understandings in the light of the ideas and experiences of others who are engaged in interreligious dialogue.

Kinds of Interreligious Dialogue

Several kinds of dialogue simultaneously contribute to the larger work of interfaith dialogue to which the InterReligious Council is committed. Let me consider three kinds of dialogue, or perhaps it would be better to say, three dimensions of dialogue. The dialogue in which we engage is intellectual, it is humanitarian, and it is spiritual.

The Intellectual Dimension of Dialogue

The word *dialogue* (from Greek *dialogos*) means "conversation." For Socrates and his pupil Plato dialogue was a technique for teaching and learning. This Socratic approach of questions and responses, of back and forth examination of a subject, of probing and weighing in the search for truth, has become a standard educational method. Teachers in Judaism and Christianity, in Hinduism and Buddhism, have all employed intellectual dialogue as a means of teaching. Such dialogue transmits religious traditions and, in some cases, persuades others to accept or embrace them. We should note, however, that when dialogical teaching occurs within a tradition the conversation partners are not always equal. The teacher, the *guru*, the rabbi, the bishop has an authority, by virtue of education and/or vocation that places him or her at a distance from the student or congregant. It is probably a good thing that students look up to teachers but there are opportunities for oppression in the teacher-student relationship. When we dialogue with traditions that have been passed down over long periods of time the weight that the official teachers give to certain doctrines or points of view may be difficult for both insiders and outsiders to appreciate. Thus there is need of dialogue both within and between traditions. As a Catholic woman I would point to my church's teaching about the ordination of women as a case in which there is dialogue within the tradition even though some of the official teachers of the church prefer to see the current practice as unchangeable. Dialogue is hindered by a premature assertion of truth. Practitioners of intellectual dialogue assume that at least some truth can be arrived at rationally and that evidence can be adduced to support religious positions. So, in the programmes the IRC conducts we expect people to bring their reasoning capacities to the conversations even as they show a respect for religious traditions that have reached conclusions different from their own.

In the work of the World Council of Churches (WCC) following First World War, *dialogue* emerged as the term to describe the interaction of religious traditions as they explored each other's teachings and practices. Later, several documents of Vatican II (1962-65) encouraged members of the Catholic Church to dialogue with the followers of other religions and to learn from their wisdom. Christian missionary activity, in which missionaries needed to know the religions of the people they sought to evangelize, forms a background to the WCC and Catholic initiatives. Among the world's religions there are today many dialogues at an intellectual level, or which include the intellectual within a wholistic approach to dialogue. The IRC contributes to this kind of dialogue in that we provide opportunities for the faith traditions in our midst to present their ways of understanding the world and the sacred and to respond to questions about them. My fellow-panelists, Jim Bresnahan and Rhea Jezer, describe some of these opportunities in their presentations.

The Humanitarian Dimension of Dialogue

Most people would say that dialogue is a good thing. It suggests a respect for others, a willingness to listen to them, and to respond with honesty and compassion. It seems to me that the ways in which those of us who serve on the Education Committee understand and practise dialogue are in accord with the approach of Martin Buber (1878-1965), the existentialist philosopher, biblical translator, and educator. In *I and Thou* (1923) Buber urged that people should not look on each other as objects (I-It) to be thought about abstractly but as fellow human beings (I-Thou) to be encountered. Thus, he held, their interaction would take place in an atmosphere of mutual acceptance. Buber believed that modern human beings were estranged from authentic existence separated from other people, from nature, and from God. He urged the recognition of common humanity and the practice of a dialogue of equals.

Recognition of common humanity urges us to care for those who are in need and, as Jim Wiggins will tell us, the IRC has been involved in several service projects on behalf of the Central New York community. The IRC mission statement says that service is one of the ways in which we "affirm the dignity of each person and every faith community."[1] Such service is, we believe, an integral part of dialogue. The humanitarian dimension of dialogue draws us into conversations about racism, about sexism, about issues of global warming and environmental degradation. In these conversations we are called on to engage, too, with those who do not embrace religion. The humanitarian dimension of interreligious dialogue includes openness on the part of those within religious communities to those who lack religious

1. The mission statement reads: The InterReligious Council of Central New York, through education, service, and dialogue, affirms the dignity of each person and every faith community and works to create relationships and understanding among us.

convictions but have strong humanist commitments. In the United States the large majority of people identify with a religious tradition. However, the American principles of the free exercise of religion and the non-establishment of religion mean that we have not only religious pluralism but also secular pluralism. You will hear from other panelists about the Community-wide Dialogue to End Racism which IRC has sponsored for the past several years and in which some 5,000 people have participated. And, you will hear about our efforts to engage people in dialogue about the environment. The humanitarian dimension of dialogue leads to action on behalf of our habitat, the earth, and on behalf of the community with which we share it.

The Spiritual Dimension of Dialogue

At the first World's Parliament of Religions in Chicago in 1893 Swami Vivekananda taught the equal value of all religions as ways to the Real and suggested the importance of shared religious experience.[2] Whether we share his notion of the Real or his understanding that all religions are of equal value is not as important as the notion that we might partake of each other's religious experience or that, while doctrines differ, there might be common ground in mystical experience. A long time ago, when I was a graduate student, one of my professors

2. The first World's Parliament of Religion was held in Chicago from 11 to 18 September 1893, during the Columbian Exposition and brought several representatives of Asian religions to address American audiences. Subsequently interest in Asian spirituality expanded and courses in comparative religion were developed in American colleges and universities. By the time a second Parliament of Religions was held in 1993 in Chicago substantial populations of Muslims, Hindus, Buddhists, and followers of other Asian religions were established in North America. A third Parliament of the World's Religions was held in Cape Town, South Africa, in 1999 and a fourth is planned for Melbourne, Australia, in 2009.

who was a Catholic and who was engaged in a Buddhist-Christian dialogue, told us of how, in one of the meetings for dialogue, it seemed that the most important accomplishment was not the intellectual discussion, as important as that might have been, but, rather, the time spent together in meditation. Dom Bede Griffiths and others who have lived simultaneously within two religious traditions have stressed the importance of contemplation and mystical experience.[3] We can hear of the religious experience of others, we can value their experience, but we go further when we share religious experiences. Members of the faith traditions represented by the IRC do participate in the religious services of other faith groups. Such dialogue requires a sensitivity to the ways in which an outsider may participate and an awareness of levels of participation reserved to insiders. We have conducted some programmes to encourage shared experience, such as one called "The Power of Sacred Scriptures" in which scriptures of several traditions were read in their original languages and then in English. A programme on Sacred Spaces is planned in which participants will visit the sacred spaces of several traditions. A sub-committee is working on a "Sacred Sounds" event in which the music of several traditions will be shared. We are still finding our way, though, in dialogue at a spiritual level. It is encouraging to see in this congress that each day begins with spiritual exercises drawn from different traditions.

Goals of Interreligious Dialogue

Basic to the work of interreligious dialogue is the recognition that we live in a world of religious pluralism. No longer in the United States are there just Protestants, Catholics, and Jews. We take note of the Native Americans who were here all along, and of the Muslims, Hindus, Buddhists, Sikhs and

3. See Bede Griffiths, *The Marriage of East and* West (Springfield, Ill: Templegate, 1982).

others who have come as immigrants in recent, and not so recent, times and have gained new members in the US. Among the goals of dialogue, corresponding to the dimensions of dialogue that I have outlined, are: learning about the world's religions, developing human relationships, and spiritual transformation.

LEARNING ABOUT THE WORLD'S RELIGIONS

Most people are relatively ignorant of religions other than their own, while, at the same time, many have a desire to learn about the world's religions. Thus, a primary goal of Interreligious dialogue is to remove ignorance, to give correct information, and to overcome stereotypes. The IRC Education Committee provides opportunities in which members of the faith communities in our area can obtain reliable information about the doctrines, practices, and history of various religions and integrate it with their knowledge of their own traditions. A concern for us since 11 September 2001, has been the ignorance about Islam. Therefore, the IRC has sought to engage the community in conversations that lead to a better understanding of Islam, its history, and its diverse manifestations.

DEVELOPING HUMAN RELATIONSHIPS

In communities across the United States today there are members of many religions. We can learn about these religions on an intellectual level, acquainting ourselves with their basic teachings and practices and history. Yet, it is when we encounter practitioners of other religions and get to know them in "I-Thou" relationships that we are most likely to come to appreciate their faith. When we go to the bank, to the hospital, to the grocery store, we interact with practitioners of many religions. It is probably in the workplace and in the neighbourhood that we have the most opportunity to engage in conversations about matters of mutual concern. A goal of interreligious dialogue is for the members of diverse religious communities to get to know each other, to find their common ground, to accept their differences, to work together. The IRC mission statement says that we aim "to create relationships and understanding" among the faith communities of Central New York. I mentioned the widespread ignorance about the teachings and history of Islam. Many Christians and Jews in the United States don't have much to do with Muslims. Thus, in the context of the US today a goal of interreligious dialogue is to enable members of other faith communities to get to know Muslims and to work together with them on common projects. I have used Muslims as an example because I think it is particularly important in the climate of the Patriot Act that we work to overcome Islamophobia and to enable Muslims to be accepted as fully participating members of the larger community. Interreligious organizations can play an important role in this work by facilitating opportunities for human relationships to develop. I should mention that the *imāms* and members of the Islamic Society of Central New York have welcomed members of the larger community to their mosque and have welcomed opportunities for dialogue.

SPIRITUAL TRANSFORMATION

It is not the work of our panel to define religion, but we can say that every religion is concerned in some way with the transformation of self and of community. The sub-title of this congress is "Can Religion be a Force for Good?" Thinking of interreligious dialogue I would also ask, "Can interreligious dialogue make us good, or, at any rate, better than we are now? Can it transform us spiritually, as individuals and as groups?" We aim at spiritual transformation through the practices of our own religious traditions. We can also aim at spiritual transformation through participating in the practices of other traditions, in shared experiences with members of other traditions, in being open to the other. We are still learning to practice our faith in a world of religious diversity and those of us who have come to Montreal for this conference have come to the conclusion that interreligious dialogue is one of the ways to do so. However, even as we say that, in broad terms, the goals of interreligious dialogue include learning about the world's religions, developing human relationships, and spiritual transformation, we cannot determine the outcome of a true dialogue. We may be surprised at where the response to the other leads us.

Problems of Interreligious Dialogue

The art of conversation may be partly a gift but it is also something to be cultivated. Certainly it is a challenge for it involves not only awareness of the self but also awareness of the other. Sometimes it requires forgetting the self in order to be attentive to the needs, concerns, and wounds of the other. The conversation of interreligious dialogue has some particular stumbling blocks. It can be inhibited by a lack of a shared vocabulary, by prejudice and arrogance, and by fear.

LACK OF A SHARED VOCABULARY

Scholars and practitioners who commit themselves to studying the doctrines of more than one religious tradition find that they tend to read the other in terms of the one with which they are first involved and that, moreover, vocabularies of the traditions may differ significantly. For example, a Christian or a Jew might come to the study of Buddhism and understand "Enlightenment" as a mode of salvation, as the end of a religious path. However, a Buddhist probably sees it as the centre of his or her religious cosmos. How can we converse when we see things so differently? The dialogues of the world's religions which have been going on for a long time now tend to neglect indigenous religions and I think it may be partly a matter of vocabulary, if not a matter of the prejudice and arrogance which we shall get to shortly. Scholars have used the language of salvation to further interreligious dialogues at an intellectual level but this vocabulary does not fit well with indigenous traditions which are deeply embedded in cultural and ecological contexts. A central notion of Australian Aboriginal religion, for example, is Alcheringa or Dreaming. The Dreaming is more an horizon of creation than an horizon of fall and redemption. The Dreaming asks of human beings that they undertake journeys along the tracks followed by spirit ancestors and continue to perform ceremonies to release life-giving power left by the ancestors to regenerate animal and plant life. The emphasis is on fertility, the power of life, the web of life in which human beings are enmeshed. Can dialogue with Aboriginal religions prompt those of us from Christianity and Judaism, for example, to find in our traditions ideas about life that would enable a conversation about the ecological crisis of our time to go forward? In Central New York it is a challenge to find the vocabulary and the opportunities to enter into dialogue with the Iroquois nations which for so long have made this region their home. It seems, though, that our dialogue will be hastened by the environmental crisis. On a hopeful note I would mention that this year a series of lectures and fora sponsored by Neighbours of the Onondaga Nation (NOON) has led a substantial number of people in Central New York to engage with the Haudenosaunee people in their quest for environmental justice.

PREJUDICE AND ARROGANCE

We all have preconceived judgements or opinions and an honest dialogue requires that we be open to revising them. In the meantime, however, prejudice inhibits dialogue. How can one cope, for instance, with the sincerely held conviction of a participant that his or her faith possesses the fullness of truth? I am inclined myself to think that each tradition possesses some elements of truth, maybe just a few glimpses of truth. In fact, I don't even find the category of "truth" that appealing.

You can see that I have some of the prejudices of the academic world and that I have a lot of work to do in order to be a practitioner of interreligious dialogue. Arrogance, an attitude of superiority, also gets in the way of dialogue. Those who are arrogant do not listen with openness because they think they know better than the one who is speaking. They are not engaged in an "I-Thou" relationship which respects the being of the other. At the outset I mentioned that a teacher/pupil or master/disciple model which has been used within religious traditions does not work so well between religious traditions. (As one who has devoted her life to teaching, I, nevertheless, have some problems with teachers and *gurus* even within a tradition. There is always the danger of arrogance getting in the way of learning.). Within a tradition the pupil is committed to receiving the wisdom of that tradition on its terms even as he or she may struggle with it. However, in interreligious dialogue the partner in dialogue is committed only to openness to each tradition's perspective.

FEAR

Fear holds us back in our life's personal and professional endeavours and so, too, it inhibits interreligious dialogue. There is a risk in reaching out to the other . . . a risk of being rejected or misunderstood. Thus, it is necessary to find a ground where dialogue partners feel at home and on an equal footing. Significant dialogue requires give and take and a long-term commitment in which fear can be gradually overcome. In our Central New York community I think, again, of Muslims after 11 September. They have been courageous in entering into dialogue and the IRC has had a role in enabling them to do so.

Those of us on this panel and those who have come to listen to us are engaged in multiple conversations about religion . . . conversations that proceed at the intellectual level, the humanitarian level, and the spiritual level. My colleagues and I are sharing with you a dialogue which is rooted in Central New York in the work of our Interreligious Council. It is, though, a dialogue which resonates with dialogues around the globe and with our conversations here in Montreal.

References

Coward, Harold, *Pluralism: Challenge to World Religions*. Maryknoll, NY: Orbis Books, 1985.

———, *Pluralism in the World Religions: A Short Introduction*. Oxford: Oneworld Publications, 2000.

Eck, Diana L., *A New Religious America: How a "Christian Country" Has Now Become the World's Most Religiously Diverse Nation*. New York: HarperSanFrancisco, 2001.

Griffiths, Bede, *The Marriage of East and West*. Springfield, IL: Templegate, 1982.

Hick, John, ed., *Truth and Dialogue in World Religions: Conflicting Truth-Claims*. Philadelphia: The Westminster Press, 1974.

Lochhead, David, *The Dialogical Imperative: A Christian Reflection on Interfaith Encounter*. Maryknoll, NY: Orbis Books, 1988.

MacDonald, Mary N., "Mission as Dialogue? The Encounter of Christianity and Melanesian Religions," *Bulletin, Vatican Secretariat for Non-Christians* XXI/I 61, 1986, pp. 269-80.

McGraw, Barbara A. and Jo Renee Formicola, *Taking Religious Pluralism Seriously*. Waco, TX: Baylor University Press, 2005.

O'Neill, Maura, *Women Speaking, Women Listening: Women in Interreligious Dialogue*. Maryknoll, NY: Orbis Books, 1990.

Sharpe, Eric J., *Comparative Religion: A History*. London, 1975.

Smart, Ninian, *A Dialogue of Religions*. London: SCM Press, 1960.

Wiggins, James B., *In Praise of Religious Diversity*. New York: Routledge, 1996.

11

Overview of the Interreligious Council of Central New York

Rabbi Daniel A. Jezer

WITHIN a few days of September 11th leaders of the city of Syracuse and county came together to plan a memorial service, urgently needed by the population. The IRCCNY was asked to play a central role in organizing this event, and on that evening, thousands gathered in the city centre as clergymen of all stripes, dressed in various vestments came together in grief and in solidarity, sharing readings from various traditions, mindful of the particular sensitivities to the many faith traditions present.

Liturgical gatherings or worship is not a focus of IRC. When IRC was founded in 1976 the name chosen defined the council as "interreligious," not "interfaith." Two concerns predicated this choice. The first was that it was felt that the word "faith" entails an emphasis on worship. The prime focus of the organization was to be education and dialogue, not worship. This has remained a constant over the years. Rarely, in its history, has IRC sponsored worship, and when it has, at times, it increased divisiveness amongst the various bodies, not harmony.

Interreligious also, as understood, referred to judicatories, the organizational bodies of the various groups. Early on it was decided that it would not be a general membership organization, but rather an organization of institutions, judicatories and individual congregations. In the past few years, reflecting changes in the landscape, both the name decision "interreligious" over "interfaith" and the emphasis on organizational membership rather than individual members is under review.

IRC, or SAIC as it was first known, was a creation of leaders of the RC, brimming with enthusiasm of the Vatican II era, the mainline Protestant organizations, and leaders of the Jewish community. At first, its Board and leadership were the leaders of the various religious bodies, the bishops, religious executives or their designees. Within a short time, this arrangement did not work, and a general BOD was formed, the membership of which represented a wide swath of the community. The Judicatory heads now constituted a cabinet of religious leaders. This cabinet has now doubled in size and incorporates about 25 leaders of various traditions, and several organizations associated with religious bodies. The BOD functions as any BOD. The cabinet has had several roles over the years, and has on numerous times redefined its role. One role has consistently been valued by the members of the cabinet and that is the ability to get to know each other, to develop personal relationships among the leaders. This has led both to individuals doing programming together outside of IRC and has aided the ability of leaders to speak with each other in times of tension between groups. Some board members see this as the single most important function of IRC. Neither the cabinet nor IRC in general has been successful in reaching out in a significant way to the religious right which is a rapidly growing segment of the religious community.

From its inception, partially inherited from the Protestant forerunners of IRC, direct services and advocacy have been integral to the workings and perhaps to the mission of the council. This was stressed and inculcated into the fabric of the organization by Dorothy Rose. She became executive director within a year after the inception of IRC and guided it with vision for 22 years until her retirement.

Chaplaincy and refugee resettlement programmes were present from the very beginning, as they were part of the Protestant council that folded into IRC. IRC contracts with various facilities around the county to provide, train and supervise chaplains, each of whom needs to be sensitive to interfaith issues. The Refugee programme has settled upwards of 5,000 persons in the Central NY region. In doing so, it has enlisted the aid of many churches to provide furniture and manpower needed to welcome these newcomers into the community.

The Refugee programme also spawned off the S.E. Asia Center, both of which reunited and morphed into the Center for New Americans. Refugees from the Mong people, Laotians, and Vietnamese settled in Central NY. IRC established a S.E. Asia Center for them to help integrate them into the community as well as to help them retain their culture. In S.E. Asia these groups were antagonistic against each other. Here, through the work of IRC, the same people were able to work together, maintain and celebrate their cultures, and hopefully model for others the ability to overcome long-standing ethnic and religious strife. Within this past year an expanded Center for New Americans was opened incorporating all this work and expanding it to better serve refugees from all parts of the world.

The direct services provided by IRC expanded over the years. It helped develop the Food Bank and the Interreligious Food Consortium, both of which spawn off. Other programmes such as Senior Home Companion, Ombudsman for Long Term Facilities, and a Covenant Housing programme for people with special needs were developed. Although these programmes do more or less involve volunteers from various faith traditions, there has been an ongoing discussion as to whether these programmes are inherently necessary as part of the mission of IRC. The question is asked if these programmes, because they are run under IRC auspices are unique, or could they be run under different auspices. Do they foster interreligious understanding in any meaningful way, or was and is the prime reason for their being under IRC financial control?

Finances, to no one's surprise, is a major issue. The core programming of IRC, that of education and dialogue is not funded. Most of the budget of some 2.5 million dollars is generated by contracted services. The core budget, which includes education and dialogue, which is not funded by contracted services, is about $250,000. Fundraising, even though extensive, cannot itself sustain this core. IRC relies extensively upon the overhead line of the contracted direct services budgets to help pay for the education and dialogue work, the essential mission of IRC.

Perhaps, a foundational faith statement which underpins the work of IRC is that dialogue is a way of affirming the dignity of each human being. By mutually exploring issues, IRC avers that respect for one another will grow. Proper contextualization is needed for dialogue, and not two monologues passing each other. We have yet to find how to contextualize dialogue on abortion and the Middle East issues, and they have therefore been avoided for fear of causing more damage. A vision for IRC was to construct a Center for Public Dialogue and to that effect a year-long dialogue programme on Visions of a World for Our Children was held. That became the forerunner of a programme that was formed 12 years ago and has become a critical programme for IRC and for the community, The Community-wide Dialogue to End Racism. From its earliest inception the pernicious issue of racism was on the agenda as a religious issue. No issue in the USA more systematically denies the sacredness of each human being as does racism. Albeit on the agenda, for many years, relations between the organization and the Black community were strained. In 1994 IRC began to seriously work on a Dialogue whose goal would be to address the issues of racism and make changes within the community. Some African-American leaders were suspicious of the idea and were reluctant to engage. They expressed the concern that this was another attempt of white people to relinquish their guilt on the shoulders of the pain felt by Blacks. Preparation for this programme was arduous and took two years and entailed scores of participants. The programme, which Jim Wiggins, our illustrious executive director will discuss in greater detail, has carried the work of dialogue and education affirming the dignity of all people to a higher level. Over the past 10 years the programme has had 5,000 participants.

Looking back over the past five years, since 9/11, or the past 30 years since its inception, the work of IRC has not significantly changed. Programmes have come and gone, names have changed as objects of suspicion and hostility. Since 9/11 the Islamic members of our community have garnered more of our attention as they are looked upon with suspicion and at times harassed, and IRC has given that group support as it has to other groups at different times. We now use liturgical occasions of worship services within individual houses of worship to attempt to foster understanding and respect for one another, especially in time of heightened rhetoric and suspicion. I have distributed two readings that we gave to houses of worship to use, one during the discussions and debates prior to the beginning of the war in Iraq, and the second in commemoration of the 5th anniversary of 9/11.

Since 9/11 the world has become more fractious, divisive, suspicious, and hostile and the work, emphasizing the dignity of each individual has become even more vital. The statement reads "The Interreligious Council of Central New York, through education, service and dialogue, affirms the dignity of each individual and every faith community and works to create relationships and understanding among them."

12

Ecology and Religion

Rhea Jezer

RELIGIOUS leaders are increasingly becoming aware of the necessity to respond to the environmental challenges of the world as it becomes hotter, stormier, unequal, crowded, more violent, and less biodiverse.

The Association for Religion & Ecology defines "Ecology" as the relationship between all species (especially humans) and the natural environment. Many people view the environment as an object to be manipulated or exploited for our benefit rather than experiencing it as the global collection of life-giving and sustaining ecosystems. Humans possess the ability to utterly devastate the environment. We also have the ability to understand the impact we make on the environment, and to make choices that lessen and eliminate ecological destruction.[1]

The "Hot topics" series of the IRC (InterReligious Council of Central New York), recognizes that religions need to be in dialogue with other disciplines (e.g. science, ethics, economics, education, public policy, gender) in seeking comprehensive solutions to both global and local environmental issues.

As part of the Oasis series, IRC is including a session on ecology and religion.[2] I will be presenting one of the classes,

1. http://www.arecology.org
2. http://www.oasisnet.org/syracuse

which is intended to explore critical issues from different religious perspectives in order to broaden understanding of the complex nature of current environmental concerns.

Until some time back, religious bodies failed to address environmental problems in a disciplined manner. It is relatively recently that religions have taken on accountability for failing to address environmental racism and injustice, unsustainable development, misuse of resources, population-consumption explosion, and human-induced climate change and global warming.

Unfortunately, in our world today, wild places which teem with wildlife, intricate ecological systems and diverse plant life are called "undeveloped." An evolutionary process which took about 3500 million years to achieve is annihilated in hardly a fraction of the time it took to create it. As religious leaders it is our duty to redefine our purpose as humans on earth.

If we take seriously the premise that we are stewards of the earth, we then must take the next step: what can we leaders, teachers, and individuals of faith do? How can we be more responsible to protect our God-given environment for ourselves and future generations? As more and more environmentally conscious people of faith are aware of how we, as individuals and members of congregations, can act and not just talk about being environmentally conscious, groups and organizations are being formed. To name just a few: Association for Religion & Ecology, Eco-Justice Ministries, COEJL, Interreligious Power and Light, National Religious Partnership for the Environment, and many others.[3]

The most prominent concern right now among all these groups and people who are taking environmental concerns seriously is energy consumption and global warming. Indeed, religious groups, such as the United States Catholic Conference

3. http://www.eco-justice.org, http://www.coejl.org

of Bishops, National Association of Evangelicals and National Council of Churches, have joined with scientists to call for action on climate change under the National Religious Partnership for the Environment which has stated, "Global warming is a universal moral challenge."[4] In Philadelphia, on Sunday, 8 October national leaders of the Muslim, Christian and Jewish communities will address the question: "God — or Global Scorching?" as part of a gathering to share in celebrating the Muslim month of Ramadan and the Jewish festival of Sukkot.

When people, and particularly religious leaders, show concern about global warming, it is hoped they ask, "what can I do to help solve the problem? What strategy can I use to minimize climate change?" The same suggestion comes up repeatedly — "replace your light bulbs with compact fluorescent bulbs." We sit here as religious leaders, dealing with complex theological issues, and all these groups can come up with is replacing a light bulb? Perhaps, but this becomes a religious issue if we leaders take it as our responsibility to promote ecology in our homes, workplaces and places of worship. Changing old-style, inefficient incandescent bulbs and putting in high-efficiency fluorescents is one of the easiest and most cost-effective steps that we can take to reduce energy use, and thus cut the production of greenhouse gasses.

To prove the effectiveness of activists, I would like to refer you to Tallahassee, Florida.[5] A proposed coal burning power plant is slated to be built there. Those who opposed it pointed out that, if all light bulbs in the city buildings were changed to the power saving kind, they would not need a new polluting

---

4. http://www.nrpe.org
5. http://www.environmentflorida.org/newsroom/clean-air-news/clean-air-news/groups-oppose-huge-coal-plant-near-everglades

plant. Hopefully they will accomplish that and stop the polluting plant. If we were successful in changing to efficient light bulbs in every house of worship in the country, one can only guess how much less energy production we would need. There is an organization which is promoting just that.

The Interreligious Power and Light, an organization which I am actively working on as the representative of IRC, provides incentives for places of worship to do an "energy audit" through the state.[6] An expert comes in to the building (or home), surveys and suggests improvements, including energy efficient light bulbs, to make the building more energy-conscious. Such things as caulking around windows and doorframes to reduce loss of heating and cooling, placing shade foliage in key points to reduce sun rays, replacing old refrigerators, appliances, furnaces, boilers and in some cases computers and monitors with more energy-efficient models, are just some of the suggestions often offered.

It is important to point out that there are many other environmentally sound practices that can be included in our places of worship, homes, and workplaces. Recycling has finally caught on in most places, reducing the need for landfills which produce methane gas. But it is important that recycling efforts be promoted and monitored.

Another serious environmental health issue is the pollution of ambient air. Walk into a building that has several computers, TVs, radios and other electronic equipment such as land phones, faxes, copy machines, add the use of sprays and pesticides, and although the chemical compounds emitted from each of these are low, the "cocktail" effect of the polluting chemicals is potent and can have a very adverse effect on our health. The offices of IRC, as an example, has a serious ambient air problem which they are attempting to deal with.

---

6. http://www.nyipl.org

I was interested but not surprised when I looked over the programme for the conference for this week. Environment or Ecology was mentioned only once, and the context was not anything I have mentioned here. As I mentioned in the beginning of this presentation, IRC recognizes that religions need to be in dialogue with other disciplines.

All major religions view stewardship of the earth as a moral obligation, and many have issued official expositions on the environment. But relatively few people make it a ministry to work for public change and to educate the folks in the pews. That has been steadily changing, along with awareness of the ties between ecology and religion. IRC, through its programming, is planning to do its part as well.

As IRC gathers people in a room, we always stress that it is a time for sharing and to show how faith traditions lead us to our positions. We attempt to explore the relationship between religion and the environment, between Creator and creation. We encourage our members to re-read the holy books from each of their traditions with a fresh ecological awareness and to interpret them contextually in the light of modern scientific advances, archaeological findings, and sociological and literary interpretation. The make-up of our membership is not necessarily scholars, and it is not only the text we seek to discuss, but we are hoping that new insights will expose how much scripture has to offer as a guiding resource for life with the rest of nature. In order to help in this deepening environmental challenge, we are hoping by our programmes to encourage places of worship and people of faith to begin to foster earth-keeping habits encompassing all phases of life including liturgy, work, leisure and politics.

13

The Work of the Education Committee of the InterReligious Council of Central New York

Rev. James C. Bresnahan

IT FALLS to me to describe for you the educational offerings of the InterReligious Council that relate to our primary objective, which is to bring people of different faiths, cultures, and ethnicities into situations of mutual respect and trust in which they can appreciate what others are saying and experiencing.

My name is Jim Bresnahan. I'm chair of the Education Committee of the InterReligious Council of Central New York, having assumed this position in retirement after forty years of work as a Lutheran pastor in Central New York.

We on the Education Committee go about our interfaith work in a diverse community. Our community is religiously diverse — Christian, Jewish, Muslim, Hindu, Buddhist, Sikh, and otherwise. Our community is racially and ethnically diverse — home to the Onondaga Indian Nation; home to many African Americans and to other descendants of those who came here generations ago; and home also to a continuing inflowing of refugees from many continents. Our InterReligious Council has settled many of these refugees.

We, further, go about our interfaith work benefiting by Syracuse University's Department of Religion and LeMoyne

College's Religious Studies programme; benefiting by the Syracuse branch of the national OASIS programme, which provides educational programmes to adults aged 50 and over; and benefiting by the regional offices of many religious bodies that are located in Syracuse or its suburbs.

Both opportunities and resources, then, for interfaith and interracial work are abundant in our community.

The Education Committee of the InterReligious Council seeks to create and foster dialogue in this setting. We do this, as Dr Mary MacDonald expressed it, with a threefold concern — for the intellectual, for the spiritual, and for the humanitarian. Or we might say, for the engagement of the mind, the spirit, and the heart. We are deeply aware of how all three need to be held together and need to work together.

We have sought to represent mind, spirit, and heart, both within the composition of the Education Committee itself and in our programming.

Nine people serve on the committee along with the organization's executive, Dr James B. Wiggins. Five of the ten have been or are university or college faculty and bring to the committee a passionate concern for intellectual integrity and rigour; all members of the committee are practising members of faith communities, four of them leaders of faith communities; together all bring to committee discussion and planning a concern for spiritual life, both individually and corporately expressed. And all members are committed to engaging others respectfully on the basis of our common humanity and for the betterment of our community and world. Mind, spirit, heart — they are inseparable within our committee, as they are inseparable in our committee programming, and inseparable in the work of the IRC overall.

I want to speak now about the work of our Education Committee, beginning with our latest endeavour related to race.

In the spring of this year, the Education Committee conducted a three-part programme for a general audience on the Aftermath of Hurricane Katrina. We approached the subject in consideration of mind, spirit, and heart by including professors offering scholarly analysis, those directly affected, and humanitarian responders from different faith communities. Presenters reflected on dimensions of loss, practical and theological responses, and the factor of race played before, during, and after the storm.

The InterReligious Council 's major effort regarding race is being accomplished not through the work of the Education Committee but through our organization's Community-Wide Dialogue Circles on Race.

Ten years ago, aided by a grant, the InterReligious Council initiated a programme of community-wide dialogue circles on race, in which inter-racial groups of about twelve people agreed to meet six times in successive weeks to work through a well-planned process. Participants engaged each other both on the level of their common humanity and with regard to matters of race that have separated and divided them and afforded whites privilege. The programme was enormously successful, such that, when grant money ended, local fund-raising has supported the continuing of the programme to this day. Already 6,000 adults from all sectors of the community have participated in these dialogue circles on race. In addition to adult participants, many high school students, drawn from urban and suburban schools, have been brought together as participants in circles.

The Education Committee is currently assisting the programme by identifying and enrolling religious leaders in dialogue circles, in the hope of bringing about significant and ongoing interactions between the faith communities they lead.

The greater part of the work of the Education Committee is devoted to promoting interfaith understanding. Recently, in a series of programmes about *Sacred Stories*, participants experienced the power of the sacred texts of other traditions, as they were read aloud by practitioners of those traditions. Building on an earlier programme called *Journey into Openness*, a new endeavour named *Sacred Spaces* commences this coming Saturday and offers a continuing series of events in which participants visit the spaces of various faith communities for a presentation and discussion. *Sacred Sounds*, to begin in the fall of 2007 and to be held annually, will bring together a thousand or more people of varied faiths to hear the music and other sacred sounds of the many religious groups in our community. It is patterned after the Interfaith Concert held annually in Washington D.C. Not in any sense a worship event, *Sacred Sounds* will, nevertheless, offer people the opportunity near our national day of Thanksgiving to join together in expressing gratitude for our diversity. Another contemplated series of programmes is *Sacred Silence*, an exploration of the ways silence functions in different religious traditions to draw us nearer to the Divine.

One of the challenges facing interfaith organizations is how to involve young people in interfaith experiences so that as adults they may be both more understanding of others' spiritual paths and committed themselves to interfaith work. Our planned annual *Sacred Sounds* programmes for the general community will be offered at little or no cost in order for large numbers of youth to participate. We are also planning a series of programmes called *Opening Doors to Youth*, in which various religious communities welcome youth of other faiths at one of their religious rites, offering interpretive commentary during the ritual experience and holding a reception afterwards with conversation.

Monthly gatherings for people of faith resume this September to discuss matters of common importance from their own religious and faith perspectives. The new series is called *Faith Views* and begins with the topic of ecology, perhaps followed by the suggested topic of religion and violence. Participants are invited to share how their own tradition has shaped their understanding of and response to whatever issue is under discussion.

Also resuming soon is a monthly reading group of interested people. First to be read and explored will be the book *The Dignity of Difference*.

Through the work of the Education Committee, the InterReligious Council has entered into a formal partnership with the local affiliate of OASIS, which provides a wealth of educational courses to adults over 50. Last year alone, thousands of older adults took courses offered by our area OASIS programme. Our first educational offering through OASIS, which we expect will attract a hundred registrants, consists of a seven-session series of two hours each on Abrahamic traditions. After an introductory presentation on the role of faith communities and religious organizations in our world, each of three major faiths will be reflected on from the perspectives of a scholar and of a practitioner/ leader. Other faiths will be explored in future offerings. Also to be offered are multiple series on *Current Issues in Religion*, with sexuality and ecology the first to be explored. Each issue will be addressed from multiple faith perspectives. Also being planned as IRC offerings through OASIS are journeys to significant religious sites of different faith communities, such as monasteries and shrines.

The InterReligious Council conducted a major conference on the theme *Power and Powerlessness in Light of the Holocaust* many years ago, in which three Christian and Jewish scholars on national reputation were presenters. Another major conference on Religious Diversity is planned for 2008 to honour our Executive Director, Dr James Wiggins, for his achievements as scholar and leader. Again scholars of national reputation will be involved as keynoters.

Moreover, there has been discussion recently within the Education Committee regarding how the InterReligious Council may be a resource to schools, corporations, and government in dealing with issues bearing on religion, such as dress, time and place for ritual observances, and religious conflicts.

I should also mention how the InterReligious Council not only promotes its own programmes, but through its e-mail service has become a funnel for promoting others' events that are of religious interest and significance. Many in our community may receive one, two, or three e-mails from the InterReligious Council , on any given day, which passes along news of significant educational opportunities that accord with its goals of creating understanding and harmony. Our organization's growing database is aided by the co-operation of area-wide religious bodies represented on the cabinet of the InterReligious Council that help keep e-mailing lists current.

Lastly, the Education Committee is charged with assisting in the planning and conducting of educational opportunities, such as retreats, for the governing board of the InterReligious Council itself, with one aim being to engage board members themselves in interfaith dialogue.

Panel No. 2
Responsibility Beyond Borders

14

Our Responsibility for Each Other

Jehan Bagli

THE cataclysmic event of 9/11 is history. It is for humanity to ponder, over how one can prevent a recurrence. The question is, are we on the right path for this quest? This event has not just cost some 3000 innocent lives, but in the five years since we have sacrificed much more than 3000 lives and has unleashed a string of death and destruction around the countries on our planet.

It has basically disconnected and fragmented the human brotherhood, a fragile entity to start with. It is always easy to demonize and caricaturize others, if the person belongs to a different race, religion or political affiliation. However, it demands courage, renunciation of human ego, desertion of hatred and vengeance, to enter in a *dialogue across the real disagreements and differences* to find and *strengthen the common grounds*, to clear the delusions, bridge the discord, to repair and restore the *oneness of the human brotherhood.*

The book *Fostering Dialogue across Divides* states:

> Dialogue can build bridges across divides in the body politic. It can promote healing in small communities that are struggling with a controversy. It can also reduce the likelihood of gridlock in the halls of Congress, hatred in the arena of public opinion, and potentially dangerous misrepresentations in our . . . media.[1]

---

1. M. Herzig and L. Chasin, *Fostering Dialogue Across Divides* (Watertown, MA: Public Conversations Project, 2006), p. 13.

Creation, according to Zarathushtrian theology, is sacred, and mankind is a crucial component of the *creation as a whole*. This ideal creation, of corporeal existence, has been soiled by the deceptive thinking of a few among mankind. However, it is the duty, function and the responsibility *of all mankind* to repair the damage that has been inflicted, and to return the corporeal, to its pristine state.

Humans are the stewards of the creation, and co-workers of the Creator. Mankind must leave no effort unexplored, to exercise their responsibility, to *refresh and renovate* the world to its pristine state as Zarathushtra stated,[2] or to bring the "*kingdom of heaven on earth*" as pronounced in Christianity, or to "*Repair the world*" as they say in Judaism. Manifestation of Divinity must be realized, through the benevolent actions of mankind, to restore the Good Rule, *Khshthravairya* in this world. That is our responsibility, that is our commitment, that should be our *dharma*.

Among the diverse cultures in this global village of ours, there is one common weakness. They all have pockets within that are intellectually weak, and economically poor, that are often exploited. Looking after the needy and less fortunate is indeed an essential part of our human responsibility to preserve the oneness of the human brotherhood.

Teachings of Zarathushtra direct all mankind to lend unflinching support for the ethical principal of justice. This is firmly enshrined in one of the simplest yet the most profound hymn known to all Zarathushtis as *Ashém vohû* meaning *Justice is Love*.

ashém Vohû vahishtém astî,
ustâ astee, ustâ ahmâi,
hyaat Asâi Vahishâi ashém.

---

2. Ys 30.9.

Simply interpreted:

> *Justice is Love. It is the Greatest Enlightenment.*
> *Radiant happiness comes to the him who*
> *Is Just for the sake of the Absolute Justice.*

This concept is also reiterated in other traditions. For instance, *Deuteronomy* 16.20 states:

> Justice you should pursue in order that you may keep alive. . . . And in the sight of God, Baha'u'llah asserts, justice is "*the best beloved of all things*."

To heal the wounds of those affected by the trauma, be it caused by a catastrophic event, or through a misfortune of nature, each one of us must accept his or her share of responsibility of repairing the harm that is done in a conflict. It is, however, crucial that the victims be at the focus of this restorative process.

We must attempt to evolve restorative justice not only for minor conflicts, but to cover the differences and disagreements between communities and nations. Restorative rather than retributive justice must be the order to address the consequences created by an act of violence, to repair as much as possible the damage that was inflicted.

As Mark Umbreit states,

> Restorative justice . . . holds offenders directly accountable to the people they have violated, providing a range of opportunities for dialogue, negotiation and problem solving, which can lead to a greater sense of community safety, social harmony and peace for all involved.[3]

---

3. "Definitions of Restorative Justice." *Hon. Marianne E. Becker Fund Incorporated*. Hon. Marianne E. Becker Fund Incorporated. 30 August 2007 <http://www.beckerfund.org/definitions.html>. Mark Umbreit is the founding director of the Center for Restorative Justice.

It is a simple wisdom that views conflicts as an opportunity for a community to learn and grow. Victims, offenders and communities actively participate in devising mutually beneficial solutions, and implementing them to restore harmony in the relationship between community members, and permits people to continue to live together in a safer, healthier environment, by exercising the responsibility to repair the harm caused by the conflict.

This is a mode of justice that demands courage and strength as a means to rebind — to *re-legio* — the community and through it the oneness of humanity. Globalization calls for the re-connectedness and for the coexistence of diverse cultures, religions and peoples. Zarathushtra offers an important guidance in this matter when he states:

Hear with your ears the highest truths and
with illumined minds weigh them with care.

Before you choose which of the two paths to tread[4]

Zarathushtra stresses the encounter of an individual with the Divine, as well as with his fellow human beings. This enables each one of us to make their own judgement about their relationship to the ultimate reality at their own personal level.

Diverse religious traditions express their spiritual sentiments in diverse ways. However, these differences should not and must not separate us in our concern for those who are oppressed, those crushed under poverty, and those stressed by the violence of catastrophe and of wars.

Every religious tradition, in its own way, teaches us to extend care beyond one's personal self. There is a concealed imperceptible component in each one of us, which belongs to the Universe at large. Mankind must learn to radiate the

4. Ys 30.2.

goodness of that Spirit to their family, to our friends, to our community, through the villages, to the nations and to the entire human race.

So long as nations will continue to use the slogan, "it is not in our national interest," there will *always* be poverty, injustice, violence and survival of the fittest. As Einstein said, "As long as there are sovereign nations possessing great powers, war is inevitable." If it is wrong for an individual to be selfish, how can it be right for a community or a nation to be selfish? This is a principle, that our politicians need to ponder over carefully. In the words of Mahatma Gandhi, "Politics without principles is a social sin." Nations must focus their efforts to change the slogan of "national interest" to "interests of humanity for peace."

Perhaps the time is here for every major nation of the world to consider having a Department of Peace, complementing the Department of National Defence. Such a ministry can function to research, articulate and facilitate non-violent resolutions to domestic and international conflict. Such a department will be involved in finding the cutting edge solutions to wage peace and not war. Perhaps then we can fully appreciate, through political channels, the true value of that Golden Rule. The rule that is enunciated in the Gathic hymns of Zarathushtra and is also enshrined in every single major tradition that followed. Only then will humans fully appreciate how viciously endless the circle of violence is, motivated through revenge and vengeance.

All the way from *Mahābhārata*, Mahāvīra, *Talmud*, *Book of Mathew*, *Guru Granth Sāheb*, Qur'an down to the Universal Declaration of Human Rights it is recognized that the common bond of oneness among humanity can be strengthened, by treating others as we expect others to treat us.

We know this bond of oneness exists. All we need is to observe the human attitude at the time of the grief of a catastrophe. In those trying moments, it is the Divine spirit that forces the recognition of the human responsibilities; it is that Providence that melts down all anger, hatred, fear, ego, and discrimination to bring to the fore the human oneness. It readily demonstrates to the victims that through humans, the Spirit of God is with them to guide them, to watch over and to walk with them through their difficult hours.

We have a responsibility to the souls of those who died in the catastrophic event in New York, in wars in Afghanistan, Iraq and in natural disasters to root out all that divides us. The struggle of interfaith movement is the struggle to eradicate religious extremism through understanding and to preserve and protect the fundamental human rights that Zarathushtrian and other traditions extol.

To be one with mankind is to be one with God.

15

Our Responsibility for Each Other

Roshni Kasad

ROSHNI spoke on the value of engaging in cross-cultural communications referring to her own experiences of working on a year-long education project in rural Gujarat, India. Roshni grew up in an Indian household in America and had never experienced living in a village in India. She was confronted with cultural norms of village life that clashed with her Western norms on a daily basis. Roshni could not simply judge the villagers and reject them when faced with a major cultural difference because these villagers had already befriended her and welcomed her into their homes as their daughter; instead, the human connection she had established with her community challenged her to probe deeper to understand the root and the value of the cultural differences. This experience helped Roshni to not just think more broadly about the culture of Indian villages, but to be more accepting of all cultures. Interacting with and connecting to people of different cultures make us more willing to resolve conflict that arises due to differences in faith, culture, and ethnic background. The process of making a human connection with others entails the idea of seeing ourselves in others and seeing others in ourselves. Only if we try to attain this supreme human connection with every being on this earth can we hope to achieve peace and justice in our global society. Recognizing the oneness of all will compel us to treat others with justice, as we, ourselves, wish to be treated in a just manner. Therefore, it is our responsibility to actively engage in forming personal connections with communities different from our own. We do not all have the opportunity to travel to a new country, as in the example that Roshni gave. Other avenues for opening up cross-cultural communication have included letter writing campaigns among children of different nations and international exchange programmes through schools and colleges. By encouraging our youth at a young age to form bonds with the variety of people that co-exist in our world community, we will be training future leaders who will be more likely to treat others with dignity and respect, leading to a more peaceful global community.

Appendix

Universal Declaration of Human Rights by the World's Religions

Whereas human beings are led to affirm that there is more to life than life itself by inspiration human and divine;

Whereas the Universal Declaration of Human Rights, as adopted by the General Assembly of the United Nations on 10 December 1948 bases itself on the former;

Whereas any exclusion of the world's religions as positive resources for human rights is obnoxious to the evidence of daily life;

Whereas the various communities constituting the peoples of the world must exchange not only ideas but also ideals;

Whereas religions ideally urge human beings to live in a just society and not just in any society;

Whereas one must not idealize the actual but strive to realize the ideal;

Whereas not to compensate victims of imperialism, racism, casteism and sexism is itself imperialist, racist, casteist and sexist;

Whereas rights are independent of duties in their protection but integrally related to them in conception and execution;

Whereas human rights are intended to secure peace, freedom, equality and justice — and to mitigate departures therefrom — when these come in conflict with the rights themselves;

Now, therefore, on the fiftieth anniversary of the Universal Declaration of Human Rights and the fiftieth anniversary of the founding of the Faculty of Religious Studies, at McGill University, Montreal, Quebec, Canada.

The signatories to this *Universal Declaration of Human Rights by the World's Religions,* as legatees of the religious heritage of humanity do hereby propose the following as the common standard of achievement for the followers of all religions or none, on the 10th day of December, 1998, as all people are brothers and sisters on the face of the earth.

ARTICLE 1

All human beings have the right to be treated as human beings and have the duty to treat everyone as a human being.

ARTICLE 2

Everyone has the right to freedom from violence, in any of its forms, individual or collective; whether based on race, religion, gender, caste or class, or arising from any other cause.

ARTICLE 3

(1) Everyone has the right to food.

(2) Everyone has the right to life, longevity and liveability and the right to food, clothing and shelter to sustain them.

(3) Everyone has the duty to support and sustain life, longevity and liveability of all.

ARTICLE 4

(1) No one shall be subjected to slavery or servitude, forced labour, bonded labour or child labour. Slavery and the slave trade shall be prohibited in all its forms.

(2) No one shall subject anyone to slavery or servitude in any of its forms.

ARTICLE 5

(1) No one shall be subjected to torture or to cruel, inhuman or degrading treatment or punishment, inflicted either physically or mentally, whether on secular or religious grounds, inside the home or outside it.

(2) No one shall subject anybody to such treatment.

ARTICLE 6

(1) Everyone has a right to recognition everywhere as a person before law; and by everyone everywhere as a human being deserving humane treatment, even when law and order has broken down.

(2) Everyone has the duty to treat everyone else as a human being both in the eyes of law and one's own.

ARTICLE 7

All are equal before law and entitled to equal protection before law without any discrimination on grounds of race, religion, caste, class, sex and sexual orientation. It is the right of everyone to be so treated and the duty of everyone to so treat others.

ARTICLE 8

Everybody has the duty to prevent the perpetuation of historical, social, economic, cultural and other wrongs.

ARTICLE 9

(1) No one shall be subjected to arbitrary arrest, detention or exile by the state or by anyone else. The attempt to proselytize against the will of the person shall amount to arbitrary detention, so also the detention, against their will, of teenage children by the parents, and among spouses.

(2) It is the duty of everyone to secure everyone's liberty.

ARTICLE 10

Everybody has the right to public trial in the face of criminal charges and it is the duty of the state to ensure it. Everyone who cannot afford a lawyer must be provided one by the state.

ARTICLE 11

Everyone charged with a penal offence has the right to be considered innocent until proven guilty.

ARTICLE 12

(1) Everyone has the right to privacy. This right includes the right not to be subjected to arbitrary interference with one's privacy; of one's own, or of one's family, home or correspondence.

(2) Everyone has the right to one's good name.

(3) It is the duty of everyone to protect the privacy and reputation of everyone else.

(4) Everyone has the right not to have one's religion denigrated in the media or the academia.

(5) It is the duty of the follower of every religion to ensure that no religion is denigrated in the media or the academia.

ARTICLE 13

(1) Everyone has the right to freedom of movement and residence anywhere in the world.

(2) Everyone has the duty to abide by the laws and regulations applicable in that part of the world.

ARTICLE 14

Everyone has the right to seek and secure asylum in any country from any form of persecution, religious or otherwise, and the right not to be deported. It is the duty of every country to provide such asylum.

ARTICLE 15

(1) Everyone has the right to a nationality;

(2) No one shall be arbitrarily deprived of one's nationality nor denied the right to change one's nationality.

(3) Everyone has the duty to promote the emergence of a global constitutional order.

ARTICLE 16

(1) Everyone has the right to marriage.

(2) Members of a family have the right to retain and practise their own religion or beliefs.

(3) Everyone has the right to raise a family.

(4) Everybody has the right to renounce the world and join a monastery, provided that one shall do so after making adequate arrangement for one's dependents.

(5) Marriage and monasticism are two of the most successful institutional innovations of humanity and are entitled to protection by the society and the state.

(6) Motherhood and childhood are entitled to special care and assistance. It is the duty of everyone to extend special consideration to mothers and children.

(7) Everyone shall promote the outlook that the entire world constitutes an extended family.

ARTICLE 17

(1) Everybody has the right to own property, alone as well as in association with others. An association also has a similar right to own property.

(2) Everyone has a right not to be deprived of property arbitrarily. It is the duty of everyone not to deprive others of their property arbitrarily. Property shall be understood to mean material as well as intellectual, aesthetic and spiritual property.

(3) Everyone has the duty not to deprive anyone of their property or appropriate it in an unauthorized manner.

ARTICLE 18

(1) There shall be no compulsion in religion. It is a matter of choice.

(2) Everyone has the right to retain one's religion and to change one's religion.

(3) Everyone has the duty to promote peace and tolerance among different religions and ideologies.

ARTICLE 19

(1) Everyone has the right to freedom of opinion and expression, where the term expression includes the language one speaks, the food one eats; the clothes one wears; the religion one practises and professes, provided that one conforms generally to the accustomed rules of decorum recognized in the neighbourhood.

(2) It is the duty of everyone to ensure that everyone enjoys such freedom.

(3) Children have the right to express themselves freely in all matters affecting the child, to which it is the duty

of their caretakers to give due weight in accordance with the age and maturity of the child.

ARTICLE 20

(1) Everyone has the right to freedom of assembly and association, and the duty to do so peacefully.

(2) No one may be compelled to belong to an association, or to leave one without due process.

ARTICLE 21

(1) Everybody over the age of eighteen has the right to vote, to elect or be elected and thus to take part in the government or governance of the country, directly or indirectly.

(2) Everyone has the right of equal access to public service in one's country and the duty to provide such access.

(3) It is the duty of everyone to participate in the political process.

ARTICLE 22

Everyone, as a member of society, has a right to social security and a duty to contribute to it.

ARTICLE 23

(1) Everyone has the right to same pay for same work and a duty to offer same pay for same work.

(2) Everyone has the right for just remuneration for one's work and the duty to justly recompense for work done.

(3) Everyone has the right to form and to join trade unions for the protection of one's interests.

(4) Everyone has the right not to join a trade union.

ARTICLE 24

(1) Everyone has the right to work and to rest, including the right to support while seeking work and the right to periodic holidays with pay.

ARTICLE 25

(1) Everyone has the right to health and to universal medical insurance. It is the duty of the state or society to provide it.

(2) Every child has the right to a childhood free from violence and it is the duty of the parents to provide it.

ARTICLE 26

Everyone has the right to free education and the right to equality of opportunity for any form of education involving restricted enrolment.

ARTICLE 27

(1) Everyone has the right to freely participate in the cultural life of the community and the right to freely contribute to it.

(2) Everyone has the right to share scientific advances and its benefits and the duty to disseminate them, and wherever possible to contribute to such advances.

(3) Everyone has the right to the protection of their cultural heritage. It is the duty of everyone to protect and enrich everyone's heritage, including one's own.

ARTICLE 28

Everyone has the right to socio-economic and political order at a global, national, regional and local level which enables the realization of social, political, economic, racial and gender justice and the duty to give precedence to universal, national, regional and local interests in that order.

ARTICLE 29

(1) One is duty-bound, when asserting one's rights, to take the rights of other human beings, of past, present and future generations, the rights of humanity, and the rights of nature and the earth into account.

(2) One is duty-bound, when asserting one's rights, to prefer non-violence over violence.

ARTICLE 30

(1) Everyone has the right to require the formation of a supervisory committee within one's community, defined religiously or otherwise, to monitor the implementation of the articles of this Declaration; and to serve on it and present one's case before such a committee.

(2) It is everyone's duty to ensure that such a committee satisfactorily supervises the implementation of these articles.

Contributors

Bagli, Jehan, retired as Distinguished Research Fellow of Wyeth/Ayrest Pharmaceutical Research, and is currently a Research Consultant. Dr Bagli is an ordained Zoroastrian priest and was a founding member and President of Zoroastrian Association of Quebec (1968-70, 1974-76), editor of *Gavashni,* a North American Zarathushti publication, for 16 years (1974-1990), and founding editor of the *FEZANA Journal* (1988-90). He has lectured extensively on numerous religious topics at various conferences and symposia and at various Anjumans in N. America. He was invited by the Zoroastrian community to lecture in India, London, and Australia. Presently, he is Chairperson of the lecture committee of ZSO, and immediate past President of North American Mobed Council (NAMC). He is the author/co-author of three books on the Zoroastrian Faith. He has been awarded the Gold Medal of the Indian Pharmaceutical Association, and fellowships from health institutions in U.S. and Canada. In 1994 he was the recipient of the FEZANA Excellence in Profession/Business Award [*address*: Jehan Bagli, Biopharmaceutical consultant, Past President, North American Mobeds Council, 16, Dallimore circle, suite 703, North York, ON M3C 4C4 (Canada) *e-mail*: <jbagli@rogers.com>].

Bhandari, Pawittar, was born in Punjab and is a holder of four masters degrees — M.A., M.Ed. Agra; MS (Ed.), State University, New York, USA; and M.Ed. (Admin.), McGill University, Canada. He taught at Kakori Shaheed Inter College, Shahjahanpur; Ramgharia College of Education, Phagwara, Punjab, (B.Ed. classes); Government Teacher's Training College and Niger State College of Arts and Islamic Legal Studies (both in Nigeria). He also served as Senior Education Officer, Nigeria. Mr Bhandari has translated several books into Hindi and Punjabi [*address*: *e-mail*: <bhandari_pawittar@yahoo.ca>].

Bresnahan, James C., has been Chair of the Education Committee, Inter-Religious Council of Central New York and served for forty years as a Lutheran pastor before retirement [*address*: 4645 Glencliffe Rd. Manlius NY 13104 (USA) *e-mail*: <jcbresnahan@yahoo.com>].

Harrison, Susan Kennel, is a PhD candidate at the Toronto School of Theology in Ontario, Canada. She served for 9 years as a co-ordinator of the Mennonite Central Committee's student exchange between Iran and Ontario. Her research and writing focuses on the possibilities interfaith dialogue provides for peace-making [*address*: 41 Galley Ave., Toronto, Ontario M6R 1G9 (Canada) *e-mail*: <sutiangle@sympatico,ca>].

James, George A., is Associate Professor of Philosophy and Religious Studies at the University of North Texas. For the past 20 years he has been undertaking research concerning the relationship of Hinduism to environmental consciousness in India. His research is published in such journals as *Zygon*, *International Philosophical Quarterly*, and *Worldviews*. He has also contributed to the *Encyclopedia of Religion*, the *Encylopedia of Religion and Nature*, and the forthcoming *Encyclopedia of Environmental Ethics and Philosophy* [*address*: 3213 Saint Claire Drive, Denton TX 76210 (USA) *e-mail*: <James@unt.edu>].

Jezer, Daniel A., B.A., D.D.(hon), served as a Rabbi at congregations in Florida, Massachussetts and DeWitt, NY for 39 years and was Adj. Assistant Professor, LeMoyne College of Religious studies. Rabbi Jezer served on many community boards both in the Jewish and general communities and was president of different agencies. He served in different capacities on the Board of Inter-religious Council of Central New York for 15 years including as president of the board, and received several awards for community services [*address*: 7426 Song Lake Rd. Tully, NY 13159 USA *e-mail*: <djezer@twcny.rr.com>].

Jezer, Rhea, holds a Ph.D from Syracuse University, MA from Columbia University, and BA from Brooklyn College. Dr Rhea Jezer is Senior Lecturer of Environmental Policy at Cazenovia College, New York. She founded and chairs the annual "Symposium on Energy in the 21st Century," which includes speakers of national note and attracts hundreds of participants from all parts of New York and surrounding states. She is also a presenter for the Al Gore's Climate Project on global warming, and is consultant to eco-businesses and environmental groups [*address*: Senior Lecturer, Environmental Policy, Dept. of Environmental Studies, Cazenovia College, Cazenovia, NY *e-mail:* <rjezer@twcny.rr.com>].

Kasad, Roshni: earned a B.A. in Biology from the University of Delaware. In 2003, she travelled to India as an Indicorps fellow to pilot the Hands-on Science project in rural village high schools in Gujarat. Roshni is currently doing her Ph.D. in Molecular and Cell Biology at the University of California at Berkeley [*address*: 1810 Berkeley Way, Apt 8, Berkeley, CA 94703 (USA) *e-mail*: <roshnikasad@gmail.com> <roshnik@berkeley.edu>].

Köylü, Mustafa, born in Turkey, holds a D. Miss. from the United Theological Seminary, Dayton, OH, and a Ph.D. in Religious Education from the Institute of Social Sciences at Ondokuz MayMs University. He is currently a professor in Religious Education at the Faculty of Theology. He has published seven books, two of which are in English [*address*: Ondokuz Mayis Üniversitesi, Ilahiyat Fakültesi, Samsun (Turkey) *e-mail*: <mkoylu@omu.edu.tr> <muskoylu@yahoo.com>].

Lepard, Brian D., is Law Alumni Professor of Law at the University of Nebraska and a specialist in international human rights law. He is co-director of the University's Human Rights and Human Diversity Initiative. A graduate of Princeton University and the Yale Law School, he is the author of a number of books and articles relating to international law, human rights, peacemaking, world religions, and global ethics. His most recent books are *Hope for a Global Ethic: Shared Principles in Religious Scriptures*, and *Rethinking Humanitarian Intervention.* He is a member of the International Board of Consultants of the Global Ethics and Religion Forum and serves on a number of editorial boards, including for *The Journal of Human Rights* [*address*: Law Alumni Professor of Law, University of Nebraska College of

Law, 213 Law College, Lincoln, NE 68583-0902 (USA) *e-mail*: <blepard1@unl.edu>].

MacDonald, Mary N., is the O'Connell Professor of Humanities at Le Moyne College in Syracuse, New York. She has worked in adult education and done research on religion in Papua New Guinea. She holds a doctorate in history of religions from the University of Chicago. Her current research focuses on ecology and religion [*address*: Religious Studies Department, Le Moyne College, Syracuse, NY 13214 (USA) *e-mail*:<macdonal@lemoyne.edu>].

Ramaswamy, Vijaya, is Professor at the Centre for Historical Studies in Jawaharlal Nehru University. Ramaswamy's first book, *Textiles and Weavers in Medieval South India* was published by the Oxford University Press in 1985 (2nd edn. OUP 2006). Her other major publications include: *Divinity and Deviance: Women in Virasaivism*, OUP,1996; *Walking Naked: Women, Society, Spirituality in South India*, Indian Institute of Advanced Study, Shimla 1997 (2nd edition IIAS, Shimla, 2007); *Re-searching Indian Women*, Manohar Publishers, New Delhi, 2003 and *The Historical Dictionary of the Tamils*, Scarecrow Press, Maryland, 2007. Her co-edited book, *Biography as History: Indian Perspectives*, has just been published by Orient Longman in 2008. The book *Walking Naked*, won the prestigious "Best Woman Historian" award from the Indian History Congress in 2001. She is an alumni of the School of Oriental and African Studies and was a Fulbright Fellow at Berkeley in California in 1988-89. She is currently engaged in the writing of two books — *Crafts and Craftsmen in South Indian History* and *Tamil Myths and Legends* [*address*: Centre for Historical Studies, School of Social Sciences, Jawaharlal Nehru University, New Delhi - 110 067 : *e-mail*:<biyarangu@yahoo.com>].

Schwartzentruber, Paul, has a BA in English from the University of Toronto and an MA in Theology from St. Michael's College, and has been involved in developing innovative and transformative programs in adult education all of his life, most recently as Director of Marguerite Centre, a spirituality and conference centre in Pembroke. He has been an Instructor in Systematic Theology at St. John's University Collegeville Minnesota and is currently working as writer and community development worker in Canada [*address*: 102

Morrison Is. Rd. S, Chapeau, Quebec, J0X 1M0 (Canada) *e-mail*: <ironpop@gmail.com>].

Sheveland, John N., received a doctorate in Systematic and Comparative Theology from Boston College and is now an Assistant Professor of Religious Studies at Gonzaga University, USA. He is a member of the American Academy of Religion, Catholic Theological Society of America, College Theology Society, and has contributed to journals like Studies in Interreligious Dialogue, Louvain Studies, Theological Studies, and The Expository Times [*address*: Assistant Professor, Religious Studies Department, Gonzaga University, 502 E. Boone Avenue, Spokane, WA. 99258 (USA) *e-mail*: <sheveland@gonzaga.edu>].

Skye, Lee Miena, is a PhD holder from University of Sydney (2005) and a Tasmanian Aboriginal (Palawa), descended from the last "full blood" before the genocide. She writes against racism, classism, sexism and naturism (abuse of nature) in the universal academic tradition of Womanist Theology. Scholarships: Australian Feminist Theology Foundation, 2005; Women Scholars in Religion and Theology, 2008. She is currently a Post-Doctoral Fellow at the Harvard Divinity School [*e-mail*: <leemienaskye@live.com>].

Index